A Guide to the Bodhisattvas

Vessantara

Windhorse Publications

Originally published as Part 3 of *Meeting the Buddhas* 1993
Revised text published as *A Guide to the Bodhisattvas* 2008

Published by Windhorse Publications Ltd
11 Park Road
Moseley
Birmingham
B13 8AB
UK

Cover design Sagarapriya

Printed by The Cromwell Press Ltd, Trowbridge, England

Cover image: Green Tārā painting by Aloka
reproduced by permission of Padmaloka Retreat Centre

British Library Cataloguing in Publication Data
A catalogue record for this book is available from the British Library

ISBN 978 1 899579 84 6

Contents

Illustrations

Colour

Monochrome

About the Author

Vessantara is a senior member of the Western Buddhist Order. Born Tony McMahon in London in 1950, he gained an MA in English at Cambridge University. He became interested in Buddhism in his teens, and first had direct contact with Buddhists in 1971. In 1974 he was ordained and given the name Vessantara, which means 'universe within'.

In 1975 he gave up a career in social work to become more involved with the development of the Friends of the Western Buddhist Order. Since then he has divided his time between meditating, studying, and assisting the development of several Buddhist centres, including retreat centres in England, Wales, and Spain.

Vessantara is much in demand as a Buddhist teacher. For seven years he led three-month courses for people entering the Order and now gives talks and leads retreats and workshops throughout Europe and Australasia.

He has written written several books, including *Tales of Freedom, The Mandala of the Five Buddhas, The Vajra and Bell*, and *Female Deities in Buddhism*.

One

For the Sake of All that Lives

What is the noblest goal to which a human being could ever aspire? Can one conceive of anything higher than the ideal of the Mahāyāna, of gaining supreme and perfect Enlightenment, the most perfect state possible for a human being, and helping all life to reach that same exalted condition? In this book we shall see, symbolically enacted, the cosmic drama by which human beings strive along the path to realize that Enlightened state; how they plunge into the depths of the mundane to bring light to a suffering universe. For here we are concerned with the great heroes and heroines known in Buddhism as Bodhisattvas (Tibetan *jangchub sempa*).

Bodhisattva means Enlightenment Being – someone whose whole energy and interest is devoted to the attainment of Enlightenment. However, Enlightenment involves realizing that the distinction we instinctively make between subject and object is false. We then cease living alone – feeling 'this is me, in here' – and setting ourselves apart from the rest of life. Seeing things with wisdom, we understand that 'self' and 'other' are merely conceptual categories that we impose on our experience. At this point it dawns on us that it is impossible to gain Enlightenment just by thinking about ourselves.

This realization has a profound effect. It is as though we had been working on the mandala of our own mind, making it perfectly harmonious, and then realized that it could never satisfy us. It will never make us truly happy because, looking out from our mandala palace, we see beyond its vajra-wall a vast mass of suffering, extending in all directions. It is like living in a grand mansion in some Indian or South American city, in the lap of luxury, while all around are shanty towns made of corrugated iron and polythene, plagued by disease and vermin. Looking out, we may feel almost ashamed of our magnificent mandala palace. We had admired it, and thought it was finished, perfect. Now we see that it is barely started. It is a brilliant speck in a dust bowl of suffering. In a flash we understand that the mandala will be completed only when it has expanded to include all beings. Its vajra-walls – which are the walls of our hearts – must fly outwards until they embrace and protect everything that lives.

So although it literally means Enlightenment Being, the word Bodhisattva always connotes someone committed to achieving Enlightenment for the sake of all living beings. The Mahāyāna vision sees the Bodhisattva working for aeons, in endless rebirths, at the service of living beings, helping them towards Enlightenment. Indeed, a popular image of the Bodhisattva promoted by some Western writers is that he or she postpones the attainment of Enlightenment in order to continue working for sentient beings. Only when the last one has gained nirvāṇa do they allow themselves to enter its perfect peace.

This idea is inspiring if we take it as a poetic way of stressing the Bodhisattva's immense altruism and bravery, but it should not be taken literally. How *can* the Bodhisattva 'postpone his entry into nirvāṇa', as some Western writers put it? To raise a semi-serious objection: if his or her altruism is of such a high order that they conceive the idea of putting all sentient beings before them, surely the extraordinary wave of merit generated by this noble thought will sweep them instantly into full and perfect Enlightenment! Part of the faulty thinking here comes from imagining Enlightenment as a fixed state in which one settles down. It would be better to think of it as involving a dynamic process of further development in a manner which, being beyond space and time, is inconceivable to the rational mind.

This conception of the Bodhisattva is very much at odds with the emphasis on gaining Buddhahood as quickly as possible that we find in many Buddhist traditions. Their view is that as a Buddha one will have the infinite resources of the Enlightened Mind at one's disposal, and will be in the best position to render help to other living beings.

Perhaps it would help us to understand the Bodhisattvas if we considered their nature not in terms of traditional Buddhism but in those of modern science. One could see the Bodhisattvas as the vanguard of the whole process of evolution. Over millions of years life has slowly developed, assuming more complex and sophisticated levels of organization, and of being and consciousness. In the Bodhisattvas the evolutionary process becomes self-conscious. Human beings possess at least the rudiments of reflexive consciousness: we are 'aware that we are aware'. This allows us consciously to direct the process of our further evolution, or development. This consciously directed development of the mind is what we call 'spiritual development' or 'practising the Dharma'. It could also be seen as the further or 'higher' evolution of humanity. Bodhisattvas are self-aware, and work on their own development. More than this, they feel a kinship with the whole evolutionary process, and do whatever they can to foster it. In them the forces of evolution become self-aware, and then 'turn back' to encourage the further development of those aspects of life which are, as yet, blindly struggling towards the light.

The Bodhisattva and the Arhat

In Mahāyāna sūtras and commentaries, the Bodhisattva ideal is contrasted with that of the *arhat* (Pali *arahat*) – the ideal Dharma practitioner of the Pali canon. It is worth spending some time exploring the significance of this class of figures. *Araham* (literally 'worthy') is a title for those who have won complete Enlightenment. In the Pali suttas it is a frequent epithet of Śākyamuni Buddha. The Buddha's first sixty Enlightened disciples are described as *arahats*, and he sent them out into the world to wander 'for the welfare and happiness of many, out of compassion for the world, for the benefit, welfare, and happiness of gods and men'.[1] However, after the Buddha's death, the idealism of some of his followers deteriorated. They wanted to devote time only to their own Dharma practice, to putting an end to their own suffering.

It was partly in reaction to this that the Mahāyāna arose. It strongly reasserted the importance of compassion in spiritual practice. Against those whose aim was the limited one of emancipating themselves from the rounds of saṃsāra, the Mahāyāna held up the Bodhisattva as the ideal Buddhist. As we have seen, Bodhisattvas aspire to gain supreme

Enlightenment not just for their own sake, but so as to be of maximum benefit to living beings. Rather than escaping from the wheel of suffering as fast as possible, he or she is prepared to work within it, for aeons if necessary, rescuing sentient beings from the clutches of the demon of Impermanence.

The tendency to settle for second best, to lapse satisfied into a concern for one's individual liberation, was personified by the Mahāyāna in the figure of the arhat. In the Mahāyāna sūtras, some of the Buddha's great arhat disciples become almost caricatures. Men like Śāripūtra (who in the pre-Mahāyāna sūtras is one of the Buddha's two chief disciples, renowned for his wisdom) become the stooges of the sūtras, their limited views being constantly exposed in the brilliant light of the profounder wisdom and compassion of the Great Bodhisattvas. They come to represent not only a narrow approach to the Dharma, but a formalistic one – often concerned with the external trappings of monasticism. In particular they stand for literalistic adherence to the minutiae of the Vinaya, the monastic rules.

In the *Vimalakīrti Nirdeśa*, one of the oldest Mahāyāna sūtras, Śāripūtra is made to cut a sorry figure next to the Bodhisattva Vimalakīrti, who has not taken monastic ordination. Śāripūtra is taken to task for worrying about where a great assembly of Bodhisattvas is going to sit: 'Reverend Śāripūtra, did you come here for the sake of the Dharma? Or did you come here for the sake of a chair?'[2] In the same sūtra a rain of flowers falls from the sky. The flowers stick to the garments of the arhats, but not to those of the Bodhisattvas. Śāripūtra is worried because monks are not supposed to wear flowers. In this way, gentle fun is poked at those who become over-concerned with the externals of Buddhism, rather than with its spirit.

A striking example of the way in which the arhats are portrayed in the Mahāyāna appears in the *Saddharma Puṇḍarīka*. At a certain point, the Buddha announces that he has a further higher teaching to give, which he has not revealed before. At this point five thousand of the assembly who consider themselves to be arhats refuse to believe there could be anything beyond their current level of attainment, and walk out.[3]

So while the Buddha's original Enlightened disciples were men and women of tremendous insight and compassion, for the Mahāyāna the term arhat, and the people described as arhats in the Mahāyāna sūtras, represent adherence to a limited ideal. When visualized or depicted in Buddhist art they appear dressed in monastic robes, carrying the wanderer's staff and begging-bowl. In contrast to the Bodhisattvas we shall soon meet, who are visualized as eternally young, the arhats are of different ages, some of them with faces lined by long lives of spiritual struggle in the service of the Dharma.

Arhats appear in Tantric meditation, especially in the Refuge assemblies. After reading some of the Mahāyāna sūtras, some people can develop a rather dismissive attitude towards the arhats, and fail to derive much inspiration from visualizing them. When meditating upon them, it is better to think of them as the fully Enlightened historical figures described in the pre-Mahāyāna canon, headed by Śāriputra and Maudgalyāyana, rather than thinking of them as representatives of a lower ideal. They can be seen as embodiments of tranquillity – people who by dint of hard effort have purified their minds, put an end to suffering, and found the 'cool cave' of nirvāṇa. They are those who, in the words of the Pali suttas, have 'laid down the burden', for whom 'done is what had to be done, lived is the holy life.'

The arising of the Bodhicitta

What is it that makes someone capable of working endlessly to help others? No ordinary person could face the hardships, or produce the extraordinary selflessness, that would be required. What turns an ordinary person into a Bodhisattva is a profound spiritual experience, the *Bodhicittotpāda*, or 'Arising of the Bodhicitta'.

'Bodhicitta' is variously translated as Bodhi-heart, Thought of Enlightenment, or Will to Enlightenment. 'Thought of Enlightenment' does not begin to do the experience justice. The upsurging of the Bodhicitta within one's consciousness is not just an idea; it is a direct experience unmitigated by concepts. It has an absolute and a relative aspect. The absolute Bodhicitta is an experience of direct intuitive apprehension of the true nature of phenomena. When it arises one catches at least a glimpse of transcendental wisdom. The relative Bodhicitta is the upwelling of compassion which is provoked by this realization. If one sees how there are living beings suffering everywhere when, if they could but understand things aright, they could have undying happiness, one can only feel the most heartfelt concern and care for them.

Nāgārjuna, one of the most influential thinkers in the whole of Buddhist history, says that the Bodhicitta is not included in the five *skandhas*. The teaching of the five *skandhas* is an exhaustive analysis of the psycho-physical constituents of an individual being, so by denying that the Bodhicitta is to be found within them, Nāgārjuna points to its transcendental nature. In dependence upon our best efforts to practise wisdom and compassion, a spiritual eruption occurs in our psyche. We contact a force for good in the universe that is far more powerful than anything our mundane self could produce.

It is as though we had worked on making the best mandala we could, with a beautiful representation of the Three Jewels in the middle. Then, one day, as we sit devotedly admiring the picture, the whole mandala shakes, and from its depths erupt three shining jewels: gold, blue, and red, of such dazzling radiance that we can hardly bear to look at them. We do not know where they came from. We do not feel we have done anything to deserve such treasures. We feel like Śāntideva's blind man contemplating the miraculous jewel he has discovered in a dung-heap.

Similarly, in our own life we can try to develop wisdom and compassion, but we cannot will the Bodhicitta into existence within us. All we can do is work at spiritual practices that set up the conditions for it to arise.

There are many methods for doing this. First there is Śāntideva's *anuttara pūjā* or 'supreme worship'. This is a sequence of consciously developed devotional moods – a 'spiritual symphony' – usually in seven movements. It begins with salutation and worship, and is followed by Going for Refuge, confession of faults, rejoicing in merits, requesting the Buddhas to turn the wheel of the Dharma, and dedication of the merits of the practice to all sentient beings.

Another practice is the meditative cultivation of the 'four factors' of Vasubandhu, one of the creators of the Yogacāra school of Mahāyāna

Buddhism. These are (1) recollection of the Buddhas, (2) considering the faults of conditioned existence, (3) observing the sufferings of sentient beings, and (4) contemplating the virtues of the Tathāgatas.

In addition there is a practice, common in Tibetan Buddhism, known as 'six causes and one effect'. This starts with consideration of the kindness of our own mother in caring for us and bringing us up, which (assuming our relationship with her has been a positive one) develops a strong feeling of gratitude.[4] We then reflect that, according to the Buddha, our current life is just one of an uncountable number of rebirths, and in every one we have had a mother who nurtured us. So great has been the number of our rebirths that in one life or another every sentient being must have acted as our mother. We try through this method to experience our relatedness to all life, and to develop gratitude for what we have been given by all sentient beings. Next we consider how all these beings have suffered, are suffering, and will suffer within saṃsāra, and we fan the flames of love and compassion towards them all. From this is born the urge to help them all to a state of true happiness. Then we reflect on how we could best accomplish this. Examining our resources we see that they are very limited, and considering further we recognize that the most effective state from which to help liberate others from suffering is the state of Buddhahood, where we ourselves are emancipated from saṃsāra and our consciousness has developed unimaginable positive qualities. On the basis of all these reasonings (though it is not enough just to think them through, one must really take them to heart and 'become' them) arises the supreme aspiration to gain Buddhahood in order to liberate all living beings from suffering.

Yet another method is at the heart of *lojong* – the teachings of 'Mind Training' or 'Mind Transformation' which were spread in Tibet by Atīśa and the Kadampa geshes. This identifies the cause of all our difficulties and unhappiness as egotistical self-concern and self-grasping. If we were not subjectively concerned with ourselves – our bodies, image, finances, pleasures – and what *we* wanted to do, what could ever happen to upset, frustrate, or disappoint us? This self-grasping is very deeply rooted in our minds and hearts. In order to extirpate it, the *lojong* teachings prescribe the practice of 'exchanging self and others'. There are many practical techniques for doing this, depending on circumstances, but the essence of them all is to work for others' happiness without concern for one's own. An example of the kind of methods employed is the meditation practice known as *tong len* – 'giving and receiving'. In outline, this involves concentrating on the breathing while imagining that with every in-breath one is taking away all the sufferings of living beings and absorbing them into oneself, and with every out-breath one is establishing all beings in happiness through sending out to them all one's positive qualities and happiness. This kind of practice epitomizes the heroic giving and all-encompassing compassion of the Bodhisattva.

All the sādhanas described in this book are prefaced by preliminary meditations designed to engender the Bodhisattva's motivation. First one goes for Refuge, committing oneself to gain Enlightenment, and then one tries to develop the attitude of a Bodhisattva, of wanting to achieve Enlightenment for the sake of all that lives. This is usually followed by the development in meditation of the four *brahma vihāras* – states of love, compassion, sympathetic joy, and equanimity, all of which can be developed limitlessly towards all sentient beings, hence they are sometimes known as the Four Immeasurables.

Lama Yeshe went to the heart of the understanding of these visualization sādhanas when he said, 'You have heard of many deities that you can meditate on, many deities to be initiated into – Chenrezig [i.e. Chenrezi] and the rest. What are they all for? I'll tell you – for gaining Bodhicitta. As a matter of fact, all Tantric meditations are for the development of strong Bodhicitta.'[5] All the Enlightened beings visualized in Buddhist practice are perfect embodiments of the Bodhicitta. Through meditative contact, or even identification with them on the basis of the preliminaries, one creates the best possible conditions for the Bodhicitta to arise.

Levels of the Bodhisattva path

Whatever methods one uses to bring it about, the Bodhicitta can arise and establish itself within one's heart to different degrees. So Buddhist tradition describes four different levels of Bodhisattvas:

(1) Aspirant Bodhisattvas. In a sense these are not really Bodhisattvas at all. They are people who are trying to act as Bodhisattvas, keeping the

Bodhisattva precepts, but in whom the Bodhicitta has not yet arisen. They are still working to set up the conditions within themselves for it to manifest. They may have taken 'Bodhisattva ordination', and committed themselves to the Bodhisattva path, but the essential experience which would make them truly Bodhisattvas is not yet theirs.

(2) Bodhisattvas of the Path. These are people in whom the Bodhicitta has arisen, who are now following the Bodhisattva path in the true sense. The most influential of the descriptions of that path, the Daśabhūmika Sūtra, divides it into ten great stages, known as the ten bhūmis, or 'grounds'. With the arising of the Bodhicitta the 'newborn' Bodhisattva enters the first bhūmi, called pramuditā (joyful). At this point he or she makes a vow, or series of vows, solemnly pledging to be the unfailing champion and guardian of all life in its battle to overcome suffering. The Bodhisattva may compose his or her own vows, or use a formula used by previous Bodhisattvas. However they are phrased, their overall aim is well summed up in the four Great Vows commonly taken in the Zen tradition: 'However innumerable beings are, I vow to save them; however inexhaustible the passions are, I vow to extinguish them; however immeasurable the Dharmas are, I vow to master them; however incomparable the Buddha-truth is, I vow to attain it.'[6]

No human voice has ever uttered anything more heroic. Having committed him- or herself in this way, the Bodhisattva begins practising the Perfections (Sanskrit *pāramitās*). Various descriptions of these Perfections are given in the Buddhist tradition. The most common list is the set of six Perfections: giving, morality, patience, energy, meditation, and wisdom. Understanding each of them from the viewpoint of transcendental wisdom, and practising them with a spirit of infinite compassion, the Bodhisattva moves steadily along the path, progressing through the *bhūmis*.

(3) Irreversible Bodhisattvas. So daunting is the Bodhisattva's task that for a long time it is possible for him or her to break the Bodhisattva vows and fall from the path. At last, though, on arrival at the eighth stage of the path, known as *acalā* (immovable), falling back ceases to be a possibility. The Bodhisattva is now irreversible from full Enlightenment, which will

finally come about when he or she has traversed the tenth *bhūmi* – *dharmameghā* (cloud of truth) – and become a perfect Buddha.

(4) Bodhisattvas of the *dharmakāya*. This term covers two kinds of Bodhisattva. The first are Bodhisattvas who have been human beings. On becoming Enlightened they retain their Bodhisattva form to continue helping living beings. The second have no human history at all. They are direct emanations of the *dharmakāya*. Thus Bodhisattvas of the *dharmakāya* are not essentially different from Buddhas. They are simply expressions of the outward-going compassion inherent in the Enlightenment experience.

So far we have been looking at the Bodhisattva ideal in theoretical terms, seeing Bodhisattvas traversing so many stages, practising first this, then that. In the remaining six chapters we shall be meeting some Bodhisattvas of the *dharmakāya*, as they appear in Mahāyāna sūtras and Tantric sādhanas. In both sūtras and Tantras they nearly always appear as young princes or princesses, attractive and decked in fine clothes and jewellery. Each Bodhisattva is a crown prince or princess, a successor to the throne of Buddhahood. The Bodhisattvas are heirs to the great kingdoms of the five Buddhas. I hope that through meeting them we shall gain a feeling for the Bodhisattva ideal, the most sublime of all the goals to which a man or woman can aspire.

Thousand-Armed Avalokiteśvara

Two

The Thousand Arms of Compassion

Avalokiteśvara could be described as the quintessential Bodhisattva, for he is the Bodhisattva of Compassion, and compassion is the distinguishing mark of the Bodhisattva. Traditionally it is said that one way in which you can be sure that a Bodhisattva is irreversible – that the Bodhicitta is unshakeably established – is that he or she never teaches the Dharma without making some reference to compassion. It is the overwhelming upsurge of compassion – the heartfelt longing to rescue all living beings from the burning house of saṃsāra – that makes a Bodhisattva a Bodhisattva. Avalokiteśvara is the figure who embodies this compassion raised to the highest power. As the family protector, the chief Bodhisattva of the Lotus family, he represents the active manifestation in the world of the boundless love and compassion of the Buddha Amitābha.

Iśvara means lord, and *Avalokita* is usually translated as 'the one who looks down'. So Avalokiteśvara is the Lord of the Dharma who looks down with infinite compassion on any being in a state of suffering. His sphere of concern is universal.

Avalokiteśvara occupies a prominent place in several Mahāyāna sūtras. He is the central figure in the *Prajñāpāramitā Hṛdaya* (*Heart Sūtra*), where he expounds the Perfection of Wisdom to the arhat Śāriputra in a very profound but concise way. This sūtra is revered and recited in all Mahāyāna countries. In the *Śūrāṅgama Sūtra* he is represented gaining Enlightenment through deep meditation on sound. The *Kāraṇḍa-Vyūha Sūtra*, reputedly the first Buddhist text translated into Tibetan, is also devoted to him, and relates how the mantra *oṃ maṇi padme hūṃ* came to be associated with him. In chapter 24 (chapter 25 of the Chinese translation) of the *Saddharma Puṇḍarīka*, the Bodhisattva Akṣayamati offers a song of praise to Avalokiteśvara which is one of the most beautiful and moving passages in all Buddhist literature. We shall quote a section from it at the end of this chapter. As well as these appearances, Avalokiteśvara plays a minor part in several other sūtras.

As time went on, his following grew, and a large number of Tantric sādhanas were composed with Avalokiteśvara as the principal figure of meditation. As this cult of compassion flowered, Avalokiteśvara appeared in many diverse forms, until now it is said that there are 108 forms upon which one can meditate.

This proliferation of forms was only to be expected. The more an experience is explored, the more deeply it is plumbed, the more subtle variations will be brought to consciousness. In English we have hardly any words for snow. If that white stuff isn't sleet or slush then it is just snow. But climbers on snow and ice have usually read and memorized a thick manual produced by the Snow Patrol that sets out the kinds of snow that are safe for climbing, and conditions in which they are risking their necks. Similarly, the preoccupation of Buddhist meditators with the exploration of compassionate states of mind produced a rosary of forms of Avalokiteśvara.

It was particularly in the Land of Snows, Tibet, that devotion to Avalokiteśvara reached its height. There he is known as Chenrezi, and is regarded as patron and guardian of the whole country, of the whole Tibetan people, and thousands of Tibetans carried him into exile in their hearts. Indeed, they would say they had done more than this, for the Dalai Lamas, the secular and spiritual heads of Tibet, are considered to be manifestations of Avalokiteśvara. The tremendous devotion shown by Tibetans to the Dalai Lama is not simply on account of his human qualities and leadership. A Tibetan, upon meeting His Holiness, feels himself to be in the presence of the Bodhisattva Avalokiteśvara.

This devotion made the mantra of Avalokiteśvara – *oṃ maṇi padme hūṃ* – almost ubiquitous in Tibet. On approaching a remote village you would almost certainly come upon a *maṇi* wall – a low wall with the syllables of the mantra painted on the stones in various colours. This mantra is more likely to be found on the lips of Tibetan laypeople than any other. Tibetans usually pronounce it *oṃ maṇi peme hūṃ*, but it is clearly just as efficacious.[7]

Some authorities consider that exact pronunciation of mantras is important, as they claim that the sound values produce subtle vibrations that affect the mind. However, there is a great deal of evidence to show that 'mispronounced' mantras can be just as effective if recited by someone with faith and devotion. In this connection there is the oft-told story of the devotee who, through a misunderstanding, thought the mantra was *oṃ maṇi padme ox*, and chanted it wholeheartedly with extremely good results.

Three forms of the Lord of Compassion

Of the many forms of Avalokiteśvara, we can pick out three to examine more closely. First there is the form called Padmapāṇi – 'Lotus in Hand'. This is a very ancient form, often depicted standing, or in the posture of royal ease – a kind of reclined sitting position with some of the body weight supported by the left hand, which is resting on the ground. In his right hand he holds a lotus blossom, the symbol of Amitābha's family. Its three blossoms suggest that Avalokiteśvara embodies the compassion of all the Buddhas of the past, present, and future. The figure of Padmapāṇi is usually red, this being the colour of Amitābha and of the setting sun.

The two other forms we are going to look at are not red but white. This points to an important principle. Any quality of Enlightenment can come to be the focus of your spiritual practice. To put this another way, any figure symbolizing a facet of Enlightenment can move to the centre of the mandala. This is what seems to have happened with Avalokiteśvara. As his compassion won the hearts of more and more people, he moved from the west of the mandala to the centre, and his colour changed from red to white, suggesting that if one could just develop transcendental compassion then the complete spectrum of qualities of Enlightenment would be bound to unfold.

We come now to one of the most extraordinary figures in the whole field of Buddhist meditation practice. The form we see emerging from the blue sky of śūnyatā is brilliant white, standing erect on a white lotus and a moon mat, and holding to his heart the wish-fulfilling gem of the Bodhicitta. As we look, we see that the figure is surrounded by a vast aura of what appears to be white light. Looking more closely, however, it dawns on us that we are really gazing at a figure with a great many arms which form a tremendous white circle as they stretch out in all directions. Each of the arms is reaching out to help suffering beings, and from the palm of each hand a beautiful eye gazes down compassionately. Several of the hands hold implements which symbolize Avalokiteśvara's measureless resourcefulness in helping beings move towards Enlightenment.

The figure actually has a thousand arms; it also has eleven heads. These are arranged in three tiers of three, above which appears a darkly wrathful face. Crowning the whole figure is the serene red smile of Amitābha.

At first sight, this figure may strike us as bizarre. We have seen that each Buddha or Bodhisattva represents what we can become, represents our own perfected human consciousness. The Buddhas are recognizably human; we are now faced with a very different form. What can it mean to aspire to have eleven heads and a thousand arms?

We have to remember that every visualization is a guide, a gateway, to a state of mind. So what we have to ask is what state of mind this figure is trying to evoke in us. To understand this it will be helpful to look at the legend of the birth of this thousand-armed form.

Once upon a time the Bodhisattva Avalokiteśvara made a great vow that he would deliver all the people of Tibet from suffering, and help them all to gain Enlightenment. He swore that he would strive selflessly to keep his vow. He made a wish that should he ever hesitate his body would split into a thousand pieces.

He entered a *samādhi*, a profound meditation, on compassion, through which he aimed to lead all beings to Enlightenment by subtle means. After a long period of time he emerged from his meditation, only to find that not even a hundredth of the Tibetan people had been helped by his practice. At this point he became totally dispirited, and thought of giving up his efforts. Instantly his head and body shattered into pieces. In agony he called out to Amitābha, who came to his aid. Amitābha fashioned from the shattered fragments a new body with ten heads and a thousand arms, which could reach out in all directions. Then he set his own head on top. Thus Avalokiteśvara was able to carry out his work of dispelling suffering far more effectively than before.[8]

This story helps us to understand the message this strange figure is communicating to us. On one level the story illustrates how the mundane ego, however well-intentioned, can never achieve its spiritual aim. In our practice of the Bodhisattva path we can strive to help all beings, but if that striving is mixed with any degree of egotism, however subtle, then that egotism is bound, sooner or later, to lead to defeat. The ego becomes dispirited or humiliated at its failure to achieve such a well-nigh impossible task. At that point we may feel like giving up altogether. However, if our desire to help is genuine and sincere, we know that we cannot give up. So we are torn between the desire to help people overcome suffering, and a profound realization of our limitations.

If we allow ourselves to experience this conflict, irreconcilable on its own level, then something higher, something transcendental, enters into the situation. It comes to our rescue. At this point the Bodhicitta is activated in our stream of consciousness, and begins to reorganize our being. It transforms our limited viewpoint into the panoramic, unbiased vision of transcendental reality. (Avalokiteśvara's eleven heads suggest this total awareness. The heads are aware of the four cardinal points, the four intermediate directions, the zenith, the nadir, and the centre. The head of the Buddha Amitābha crowning the others emphasizes that an element of transcendental wisdom is present.)[9] Our capacity to help living beings becomes almost endless, and our resourcefulness knows no bounds.

It should now be clear that the thousand-armed figure is a symbol for a consciousness which has been completely transformed by the Bodhicitta, a consciousness whose only wish is to help beings eternally, in an infinite number of ways. It communicates to us at least an inkling of what it would be like to love the world so much that two eyes were not enough to weep for its sufferings and two arms could not begin to embrace it. Perhaps we could say that the figure is really the 'Infinitely-Armed Avalokiteśvara', for he reaches out to assuage the pains and struggles of living beings everywhere.

Consideration of the birth of the thousand-armed figure prompts some reflections about Buddhist practice in general. First, it sheds some light on the question of working for spiritual aims with mixed motives. Clearly, to work for a spiritual goal we must have a spiritual motivation. If we do not, we will almost certainly end up debasing our goal. For instance, suppose someone decided to set up a Buddhist centre simply in order to become famous, or to be the focus of an admiring circle of followers. What they would produce, even though it might be called a Buddhist centre, would have nothing to do with the Dharma. The 'taste of freedom', which is said to be present wherever the Dharma is found, would be conspicuously absent.

What, then, if one is in the position that so many of us find ourselves in, of having genuinely altruistic feelings, really wanting to do something for the world, but being uneasily aware that these positive emotions are mixed with less skilful elements, such as ambition or the desire to be noticed? What the story of Avalokiteśvara indicates is that we should not hold back from acting to help others, even if we know that our motives are not totally pure. As long as we are sure that our basic concern is to help others, and we stay aware of our tendency to let selfish motives intrude, we should just go ahead. The world needs whatever crumbs of altruism we can give it. It cannot wait for us somehow to make our motives one hundred per cent pure. Indeed, it is through the process of putting our energy honestly and wholeheartedly into an altruistic enterprise that our motives will be purified. If we simply work from the best motivation we can find in ourself at the time, then, as we persevere, our unskilful motivations will 'crack'. Bit by bit our being will be reorganized around the Will to Enlightenment.

Buddhism teaches us that to gain Enlightenment we have to go beyond, or see through, the fixed unchanging ego, with its aversions and predilections. Unfortunately this sometimes leads people to take cudgels to themselves. In their attempts to stamp out the ego, they bring themselves to a virtual standstill. Sometimes they become so suspicious of themselves, constantly spying on themselves for signs of ego, that they become negatively self-obsessed, and fail to make any real spiritual progress. A much better approach is simply to give the ego an assignment which is too big for it. It appears to be such a big fish because it is usually kept in a very small pool of mundane concerns. Ask it to undertake something genuinely idealistic and far-sighted and the poor thing becomes insecure and begins to realize its limitations. Eventually it is only too happy to retire, and pass the job over to those deeper parts of the psyche that can respond to the challenge with enthusiasm.

The dissolution of Avalokiteśvara into fragments also suggests something about the nature of the Bodhicitta. Avalokiteśvara thinks of himself as being capable of *personally* delivering all the beings in Tibet from suffering. It is only when this view cracks that something much higher supervenes. It is usual for followers of the Mahāyāna to take Bodhisattva vows, including vows such as 'However infinite sentient beings are, I vow to save them.' While such aspirations are to be applauded, there is possibly a danger. That danger is of 'giving oneself airs' by starting to think of oneself as a Bodhisattva. As the story shows us, it would be closer to the truth to acknowledge that one cannot save all sentient beings from suffering, however much one might long to do so. All one can hope to do, realistically, is to participate in the Bodhicitta to some degree, to allow it to manifest through one. 'Not I, not I, but the wind that blows through me!' must be the cry.[10] In fact, rather than imagining ourselves as a Bodhisattva taking all the sufferings of the world upon our shoulders, it would be better if we were to think of ourselves as just one of Avalokiteśvara's hands, reaching out to the world, giving whatever help and assistance we can.

Thus the thousand-armed form is perhaps a better symbol for a spiritual community, a sangha, than it is for an individual spiritual aspirant. In the Mahāyāna context, the whole sangha is devoted to the Bodhisattva ideal, but each member will work for it in his or her own way. Each person is like a hand of Avalokiteśvara, reaching out in their own life to offer their talents and capabilities; yet they also work in concert, united by their common vision, just as the thousand arms reach out in different directions. All are guided by the brilliant light from the jewel of the Bodhicitta

Four-Armed Avalokiteśvara

which the figure holds to his heart. So the figure is a perfect symbol for the blending of unity and diversity, which is the spirit that should permeate a spiritual community.

Now it is time to turn to another peaceful form of Avalokiteśvara. Apart from the thousand-armed, the most common form is that with four arms. In this figure the four arms are said to represent the four Tantric functions of pacifying, increasing, attracting, and destroying.

This form has been a favourite subject for meditation, and there are many sādhanas in which he appears. Let us try to see him in our mind's eye, as though we were performing a visualization. In this way we can meet Avalokiteśvara more directly, and allow his appearance to give our minds some feeling for the beauty and power of his boundless compassion. The meditation I am going to describe[11] is a self-visualization in which *we* become the Bodhisattva, and thereby refine the subjective aspect of the subject–object duality. It is important to understand that such practices transcend the boundaries of gender. Hence a woman may visualize herself as a male Buddha or Bodhisattva; equally a man may become a female figure. Enlightenment transcends all gender differences. As an illustration of this, Avalokiteśvara, who in India and Tibet is definitely a male figure, became transformed in Far Eastern Buddhism into a compassionate goddess. In China she is known as Kuan Yin, and in Japan as Kannon or Kwannon. Like Avalokiteśvara, Kuan Yin can take a number of forms. Perhaps the best-known is the White-Robed Kuan Yin, of which there are many beautiful porcelain statues.

Visualizing the four-armed form

First we imagine the vast blue sky, stretching in all directions, absolutely clear and radiant, the symbol of śūnyatā, the emptiness of self-nature, which is the hallmark of all our experiences. Experiencing the freedom of the blue sky, extending to infinity, we can gain a feeling for the expansiveness and freedom which could be ours if we did not allow our horizons to become limited, if we did not permit our minds to become fixated and hypnotized by cravings, dislikes, and worries centred on what are really empty, passing phenomena.

Next, out of the sky beneath us, appears a throne of jewels. Blazing brilliantly, its many-hued lights shine way off into the blueness. On top of the jewel throne appears a perfect lotus flower, and on top of that a circular mat of pure white light, like a full moon.

On this moon mat we are seated. However, something extraordinary has happened. In dwelling on the blue sky, on the lack of inherent nature of all phenomena, we intuited that there is nothing fixed and unchanging in us. All the aspects of our self and our experience are just like clouds. They arise out of the blue sky and roam across its vast expanses for a while, but eventually, however tall and mighty, they dissolve back into the blue sky. We see, with Prospero, that:

The cloud-capp'd towers, the gorgeous palaces,
The solemn temples, the great globe itself,
Yea, all which it inherit, shall dissolve
And, like this insubstantial pageant faded,
Leave not a rack behind. We are such stuff
As dreams are made on, and our little life
Is rounded with a sleep.[12]

Seeing that what we think of as ourselves is cloud-like, dream-like, evanescent, we realize that there is nothing in ourselves which cannot be transformed. In the blue sky we have let go of our old dream (or nightmare!) of ourselves as fixed, limited, and suffering. Now, awake and aware, we fashion our cloud-like existence into a finer shape. We begin lucidly dreaming the finest dream available to us as human beings. In Emptiness we let go of our old identity, and we become Avalokiteśvara, the Bodhisattva of Infinite Compassion.

So we find ourselves transformed. We are seated on the white moon disc, our legs in the full-lotus posture. Our body is made of brilliant white light, the colour of a spotless conch shell or of a snow mountain. We are adorned with jewels and silks. We have four arms. An inner pair, held to our heart, clasp the wish-fulfilling gem of the Bodhicitta, our greatest treasure. In our outer left hand we hold a lotus flower, and in our outer right hand a crystal rosary. We are surrounded by a great aura of light. Tresses of blue-black hair cascade over our shoulders. We are sixteen years old, handsome and smiling, and gazing out over the world with gentle eyes.

It is not enough simply to take on the form of Avalokiteśvara. At this point in the practice we try to identify ourselves with him completely, to generate the divine pride – as it is called – of actually being the Bodhisattva, reminding us that our old self was dissolved away into Emptiness.

Knowing our true nature to be essenceless, we sit alone in the blue sky. No, not quite alone. Looking upwards we see that, above our head, blazing like a giant ruby, is the figure of Amitābha ('infinite light'). As we have seen, Avalokiteśvara is the chief Bodhisattva of the Lotus family. He is the active expression of the boundless love of Amitābha. For us as Avalokiteśvara, Amitābha is our spiritual father, our guru, the fountainhead of all our understanding of the Dharma. So he sits in the place of honour above our head, a constant source of strength and inspiration.

As so often in sādhanas, there are many layers of meaning, some apparently contradictory, to be discovered by dwelling on the meditation as it unfolds. On one level we are separate from Amitābha. He is our guru, our mentor, the centre of all our devotion. Yet, at the same time, we and Amitābha are one, or at least not two. In a sense we are simply a manifestation of Amitābha's love and compassion. In fact, as we look into our heart-centre, the nucleus of our being, we see another smaller lotus and moon mat, and standing at its centre the blazing red *bīja* mantra, or seed syllable, *hrīḥ*. This *bīja* mantra is the same as that which is found in Amitābha's heart, emphasizing that in our core, in the fire of our love and compassion for all that lives, we and Amitābha are indissolubly united.

Standing in a circle around the seed syllable, like the stones of Stonehenge, are the syllables of the mantra *oṃ maṇi padme hūṃ*. Each syllable is of a different colour, the colours being associated with the six realms of mundane existence shown in the Wheel of Life. Dwelling on these six shining syllables, we as Avalokiteśvara gaze out, with infinite compassion, onto the six realms. As we contemplate the sufferings of sentient beings, the wheel of six syllables begins to turn clockwise in our heart.

As the mantra rotates it starts to sound. In response to the ocean of suffering of living beings: their physical pains, their hunger, their fear of death, their thwarted ambitions and frustrations, light pours out from the six syllables into all the realms. From the white *oṃ* in our heart, white light reaches out to the realm of the gods. From the green *ma*, green light goes out to the asuras. From the yellow *ṇi*, yellow light pours down on human beings. From the blue *pa*, blue light rains down on the animal kingdom. From the red *dme*, red light assuages the neurotic desires of the hungry ghosts. From the deep-blue *hūṃ*, smoky-blue light removes the agonies of those in states of extreme suffering and distress.

Filled with deep devotion to Amitābha, and compassion for the trials and miseries of all unenlightened beings, we sit in the sky like a great white cloud, empty in our essential nature, pouring down happiness on the world. With each rotation and recitation of the mantra, we count off another crystal bead on the rosary in our right hand. Each bead that passes through our fingers is a living being rescued for ever, by the power of the mantra, from the six realms of saṃsāra. As Avalokiteśvara we are prepared to pour down the light of compassion on the world ceaselessly. We are prepared to continue the practice until we have counted off a crystal bead for every single living being. We are prepared to work for however long it may take, until, looking down with loving eyes, we can find no suffering anywhere.

As he who has reached perfection in all virtues,
Who looks on all beings with pity and friendliness,
Who is virtue itself, a great ocean of virtues,
As such Avalokiteśvara is worthy of adoration.

He who is now so compassionate to the world,
He will a Buddha be in future ages.
Humbly I bow to Avalokiteśvara
Who destroys all sorrow, fear, and suffering.[13]

Mañjuśrī

Three

The Soft-Voiced Prince and the Flaming Sword

In the previous chapter, we were looking at embodiments of love and compassion, at forms of Avalokiteśvara who is a central figure in the family of Amitābha. The Lotus family has always had many devotees, because people are drawn to love and kindness. In the modern world particularly, we often hear people bemoaning the lack of love in their lives. It is a commonplace lament that there is not enough love in the world, and many people subscribe to the view that 'all you need is love'. However, there is another way of looking at things, a way which is at least as common in the Buddhist tradition. While love for other living beings is obviously very valuable, one could argue that what we need most of all is wisdom.

The search for wisdom

This will sound strange to modern ears. In the twenty-first century, wisdom has gone out of fashion. It has become degraded to the extent that it is almost synonymous with a cynical view of life, in which you do not get 'caught out'. Wisdom now lives a ghostly existence in phrases like 'street-*wise*' or '*wise* up, kid.' This modern wisdom is well summarized by Bernard Berenson, in his *Dictionary for the Disenchanted*. 'Wisdom' he says 'is the understanding that things are worse than they used to be, but better than they're going to be.'

Wisdom has gone out of fashion partly because modern life has increased in pace and in its capacity to preserve information. In traditional societies the wisdom of age was highly respected. In a stable society without access to information technology, old people were wise because they had seen and heard much. In tribal societies, the elders were the history books, the tomes of legal precedent, the living maps of the tribal lands. As life and conditions changed only slowly, their experience was relevant and useful. Nowadays, however, the great libraries and computer databases are the preservers of useful knowledge. As for the wisdom of age, this is all too often seen as old people reminiscing about a world that has ceased to exist, in which everything cost a fraction of what it does now.

As for philosophy, which is literally 'the love of wisdom', it appears all too often to retreat into the safe ivory towers of intellect.[14] If we look at the current situation, we could justifiably conclude that wisdom, like Nietzsche's God, is dead.

For Buddhism, however, wisdom is not dead. Buddhism's basic aim is to eradicate ignorance by developing transcendental wisdom. The world may not appreciate it, but it desperately needs wisdom. We have wandered so far away from it that we no longer recognize our lack. The world needs wisdom perhaps more urgently than ever before. From the Enlightened point of view, the way most of us see the world is just madness because we subscribe, most of the time, to what are called the four *viparyāsas* – the four 'upside-down views'. First, we treat what are really impermanent processes as though they were permanent and reliable. Secondly, we expect these changing processes to give us permanent satisfaction, when they are bound to fail us. Thirdly, we see these flowing processes as having a substantial, unchanging core or self-nature. Lastly, we treat the appearances of saṃsāra as though they were beautiful when they are not – certainly not when compared to the beauty of Reality. So, approaching the world in this crazy way, it is not surprising that our lives usually do not work out as we had hoped. Nor is it surprising that when we come across the Dharma we may at first find parts of it uncomfortable and hard to accept. In fact, it is a step toward wisdom when we begin to realize how far from it we have strayed.

Understanding the true situation can also make us more sympathetic to ourselves. Once, in the middle of a very intensive meditation week, I began having some quite strange and disturbing experiences. I comforted myself, and kept myself going, with the reflection that I had nothing to lose but my insanity!

As well as madness, the unenlightened state is often compared to blindness. A blind man with a stick is the image for primordial ignorance in the outer circle of the Wheel of Life, a graphic illustration of how beings create the causes of suffering. Seen in terms of this image, the world's leaders really are the blind leading the blind. However, through practice of the Dharma – through study, meditation, and communication with those who are wiser than ourselves – it is possible for us to come closer to sanity. In our blind darkness we can begin to see light.

As we cautiously tap our way along, trying to follow the path to wisdom we have heard about, we can begin to make out an area ahead that is distinctly lighter. At first it is dim and unclear, but as we approach it becomes brighter. After a while, as we move more confidently and surefootedly, it becomes a great light like the sun. This light increasingly seems to be banishing our blindness, like the sun dispelling clouds.

The light becomes even more golden and brilliant, until finally we can see its source. It is a figure completely composed of golden-yellow light. It is a young man, perhaps sixteen years old, though there is a timeless youthfulness about him. He is sitting cross-legged on a white moon mat on a pale-blue lotus throne. His well-proportioned body is adorned with precious jewels and silks. He is handsome and smiling. Blue lotuses are twined into his long black hair, below a crown of jewels. His left hand holds a book to his heart. In his right hand he effortlessly and gracefully wields a great two-edged sword with a vajra handle. Flames dance around the tip of the sword.

Following the path of the Dharma, we have been brought face to face with Mañjuśrī (Tibetan *Jampal*), the Bodhisattva of Wisdom. It was the radiance of his Enlightened understanding, pouring from his body, which led us on. Having met with him, we can contemplate his serene figure, and see what occurs to us.

Meditating on Mañjuśrī, these are some of the thoughts that have occurred to me over the years. He is youthful, because wisdom is ever new, ever fresh, ever spontaneous. He is handsome, because wisdom involves aesthetic appreciation, valuing things for themselves, for their beauty, and not trying to appropriate and use them. Wisdom is a flower that can never be picked. He is well built because wisdom bestows true strength. He sits cross-legged on a blue lotus, because with wisdom comes a serene withdrawal from the cares of the world. We may still act within it, but we no longer have expectations of it; so it no longer disturbs us. With wisdom comes total contentment and self-sufficiency.

He is said to be the colour of the sun, or of a lion's eye. The lion is his animal, and he is sometimes shown seated upon one. The lion is also associated with Vairocana, and Mañjuśrī is the protector of Vairocana's Tathāgata family. The name Vairocana means illuminator, and he and Mañjuśrī are linked by their common solar symbolism. In this respect, and in others, Mañjuśrī has certain similarities to Apollo, the Greek god of light, music, healing, poetry, and prophecy. Apollo, we could say, is Mañjuśrī's unenlightened younger brother.

The book that Mañjuśrī holds to his heart is a volume of the *Perfection of Wisdom in 8,000 Lines*. This text belongs to a very important class of Buddhist literature known as the Perfection of Wisdom (Sanskrit *Prajñāpāramitā*), which developed over a period of about 1,000 years from around 100BCE.[15] Mañjuśrī holds the book to his heart because he knows that wisdom is the most precious of all possessions.

Mañjuśrī in Buddhist tradition

Before we consider the flaming sword, the second of his two main emblems, let us fill in some background about the Bodhisattva of Wisdom in Buddhist tradition. He is known by several names, but most commonly as Mañjuśrī (gently auspicious). He is also referred to as Mañjughoṣa (gentle-voiced one), as Vāgīśvara (lord of speech), and as Kumārabhūta (crown prince).

Mañjuśrī is a figure of central importance in all countries where Mahāyāna Buddhism flourished. In Nepal, according to the *Svayambhūpurāṇa*, Mañjuśrī created the Kathmandu valley by draining the waters of a lake. He did this by opening up six valleys on the south side of the lake by cleaving the mountains with his sword.[16]

In China, Mañjuśrī was believed to turn the Wheel of the Dharma on Mount Wu-Tai Shan in Changsi province. Over the centuries, crowds of pilgrims have flocked to this high mountain range (rising to 3,040 metres). During the Tang dynasty (618–907CE) it became a centre for pilgrims from all over China and beyond. The mountain was originally a Taoist holy place. However, during the fourth century it was adopted by the Buddhists and made the home of Mañjuśrī. According to the French scholar Étienne Lamotte, the Chinese translators of the *Avataṃsaka Sūtra* inserted into the original text a passage stating that the mountain was an ancient residence of Mañjuśrī.[17] Wu-Tai Shan is interesting inasmuch as it is a chain of five peaks, and one of the titles given to Mañjuśrī in Indian Buddhist literature is Pañcacīra, which means Five Crests. He is often depicted with five tufts of hair or a five-pointed crown, and with five lotuses wound into his hair.

In Japanese Zen, where he is known as Monju, he is seen as one of the two principal attendants on Buddha Śākyamuni. As Zen is so uncompromisingly concerned with the quest for wisdom, Mañjuśrī's figure is to be found in virtually every temple and monastery.

Mañjuśrī appears in many important sūtras. For example, he plays a major role in the *Vimalakīrti Nirdeśa*. The central figure of this sūtra, Vimalakīrti, is a Bodhisattva who practises profound skilful means in order to attract people to the Dharma. At the beginning of the sūtra he appears to be sick so that people will come to visit him and he will be able to point out to them the fragility and perishability of the body. The Buddha is concerned that some of his followers should visit Vimalakīrti to enquire after his health, but finds himself short of volunteers. All the Bodhisattvas fight shy of seeing Vimalakīrti, as they have been trounced in debate by him on previous occasions. Only Mañjuśrī is willing to visit the invalid and risk having any wrong views exposed by Vimalakīrti's uncompromising transcendental vision.

Mañjuśrī's encounter with Vimalakīrti is one of the most famous incidents in Mahāyāna literature. First, various Bodhisattvas who have accompanied Mañjuśrī as his attendants are asked by Vimalakīrti to explain how one enters the 'Dharma door of non-duality', i.e. how to attain the transcendental path. When they have all done so to the best of their ability, Mañjuśrī shows them that their explanations are still caught up in subtle dualities. He then gives his own view, taking the discussion as far as it can be taken in words. Knowing there is nothing further that can be said on the subject, he deferentially invites Vimalakīrti to give his answer. Mañjuśrī's ace is then trumped by Vimalakīrti. Rather than give any conceptual explanation, he keeps a 'thunderous silence'. This silence of Vimalakīrti's has echoed throughout Buddhist history.

Mañjuśrī appears in a number of Mahāyāna sūtras of the Ratnakūṭa (jewel-heap) class, including the *Mañjuśrī-Buddhakṣetra-guṇa-vyūha*, which describes the qualities of his Pure Land. In the *Gaṇḍavyūha Sūtra* it is his advice to the young spiritual aspirant Sudhana to seek out a spiritual friend (Sanskrit *kalyāṇa mitra*) which starts Sudhana on the epic pilgrimage that is to take him to no less than fifty-three spiritual teachers. Mañjuśrī also plays a central part in the *Perfection of Wisdom in 700 Lines*. As well as the Mahāyāna sūtras, he has a key role in a number of important Tantras, including the *Mañjuśrī Mūla Kalpa* and the *Mañjuśrī Nāma Saṅgīti* (chanting the names of Mañjuśrī) one of the most important early Tantras.

Wherever and however he appears in Buddhist tradition, Mañjuśrī represents transcendental wisdom. Not only that; he presides over all intellectual development. It is said that through his sādhana one can develop knowledge and a retentive memory. He is the patron of the arts and sciences.[18] He is the 'supreme master of sacred eloquence'.[19] Traditionally, if you want to write a book, or paint a *thangka*, you invoke the aid of Mañjuśrī. He gives clarity of mind – his sun-radiance dispels the obstacles to clear understanding. In particular, he bestows the power of understanding the Dharma, and the capacity to explain it to others.

Practice of his sādhana is indicated for those whose deepest desire is to know, to understand, who are attracted by the possibility of developing wisdom and insight. It is good for people with lively minds, and those who want to develop clarity of thinking and expression.

Like Avalokiteśvara, Mañjuśrī appears in a number of different forms. According to Indian tradition there are thirteen main forms. He is usually golden yellow or orange in colour, but he can be white or, less commonly, black. Some of these figures hold the sword and book; others hold stems of lotuses that support the sword and book on their flowers, which are open at shoulder level. He also appears in a wrathful guise, in the various forms of Yamāntaka (slayer of death), of which the best known is Vajrabhairava (diamond terrifier), who is buffalo-headed and has thirty-four arms. Several figures in Tibetan religious history are considered to be manifestations of Mañjuśrī. According to Tibetan tradition the three most important are the Nyingma teacher Longchenpa, Sakya Pandita (one of the Five Masters of the Sakya school), and Je Tsongkhapa, founder of the Geluk school.

A Mañjuśrī sādhana

Now we shall look at a simple Mañjuśrī sādhana,[20] before considering the significance of that flaming sword. The sādhana begins with verses of Going for Refuge – committing oneself to the attainment of Enlightenment – and generation of Bodhicitta – developing a feeling of infinite compassion, so that even gaining Enlightenment becomes only a means to an end. We want to gain Enlightenment because we shall then be in the best position to help living beings.

Once we have established our motivation in this way, we dissolve everything into Emptiness. Next, the sky in front of us becomes lighter and brighter and Mañjuśrī appears, seated on a pale-blue lotus and a white moon mat. He is golden yellow, with long black hair, dressed in silks and jewels, holding the flaming sword in his right hand and holding the book of Perfect Wisdom to his heart in his left.

After we have contemplated him for a while, rays of light radiate from his brilliant form and invite the five Buddhas to appear in the sky above his head. Each Buddha carries a vase of initiation. They slowly tilt their vases, from which wisdom-nectar streams forth. The five-coloured nectar cascades through the blueness, and is absorbed into the body of Mañjuśrī, whose form shines even more brightly than before.

This form of initiation is based on ancient Indian ceremonies for anointing kings. A prince would be endowed with all the powers of kingship in a ceremony in which his predecessor poured water over his body from a number of jars. This symbolism was taken over by the Vajrayāna, and is much used in Tantric initiation. In the sādhana we see Mañjuśrī, the crown prince, symbolically anointed with all the wisdom and powers of Buddhahood by the five Buddhas. After the consecration, they descend onto the crown of Mañjuśrī's head, where they sit like a tiara of jewels.

Next, we develop strong devotion for Mañjuśrī, and a longing to achieve his Enlightened state. In response, a beam of light shines from Mañjuśrī's heart, down which flow the syllables of his mantra, which enter our heart. We then repeat the mantra a number of times.

Mañjuśrī has more than one mantra associated with him. In this sādhana it is *oṃ a ra pa ca na dhīḥ*. *Dhīḥ* is the seed syllable particularly associated with Perfect Wisdom.[21] The five syllables, *a ra pa ca na*, are the first five letters of what is known as the 'alphabet of Perfect Wisdom'. In this, each letter of the Sanskrit alphabet is associated with an epithet of the Perfection of Wisdom. However, one need not reflect on such things while reciting the mantra. It is enough to concentrate on it wholeheartedly, feeling that through reciting it we are deepening our links with Mañjuśrī and imbibing his wisdom. We try to feel this as strongly as possible. When we first perform the sādhana we may feel that we are engaging in make believe. With regular practice, though, this 'acting as though' becomes more wholehearted, and we experience the chasm of consciousness between us and Mañjuśrī beginning to close.

Once the mantra recitation is finished, we either visualize Mañjuśrī as being absorbed into ourself, or as dissolving away into the blue sky. After that we just sit silently, aware but without making any mental effort. All our work in the sādhana, all the visualization and mantra recitation, has been a matter of setting up the conditions for this aware letting-go. In the silence, unmediated by symbols or concepts, we aim to directly experience the message of wisdom the sādhana is trying to impart. When we get up from our meditation seat we try to carry into everyday life as much as we can of the experience of the sādhana.

The flaming sword and the wisdom beyond words

Having looked at a sādhana of Mañjuśrī, it is now time to look at his main emblem, the flaming sword. Some friends of mine in India, who are devotees of Mañjuśrī, found it necessary for a while to hide away their images and pictures of him. Word was spreading that they were 'worshipping a Buddha with a sword'. This was taken by the local people to mean that they were practising a Buddhism that sanctioned bloodshed. So why is a Bodhisattva, whose very nature must be love and compassion, represented brandishing a sword? Is not the sword a symbol of violence, which surely has no place in the spiritual life?

In a sense, any radical transformation involves a degree of violence. You can only produce a more positive self by putting paid to your old bad habits. Violence, in itself, is simply a forceful use of energy. What makes it skilful or unskilful is the state of mind which directs it. Used with hatred against another person it causes damage and deprives them of their freedom. Used with understanding against wrong views, negative emotions, and limiting behaviour it creates freedom, and the space for new growth.

Mañjuśrī's sword is directed against anything that obstructs wisdom, or causes suffering. In particular, it cuts away at all our ideas about the world. Transcendental wisdom is not concerned with producing ideas, even correct ideas. The sword of wisdom cuts away our web of concepts about life, and enables us to dive fully into life, to experience it directly.

When people think of wisdom they sometimes imagine some wise old man with twinkling eyes telling them the secrets of the universe. However, the essence of Buddhist wisdom is that it goes beyond words. The whole of the Perfection of Wisdom literature, with its paradoxical logic, is trying to shock us into seeing that our concepts of the world do not match up to the facts of experience. Buddhism does not answer your questions about life with some neat formula. Rather, it provides tools for transcending the state of consciousness in which the question was framed. The question is a product of the degree of conflict experienced at that level of consciousness.

This is not to say that one should not try to clarify one's thinking. Most of us have been brought up with a whole series of untested assumptions about life. We absorbed them from our parents and teachers at an age before we were able to consider them critically. We have held them for so long that they have become our mental wallpaper; we take them for granted. So it is a useful beginning to the quest for wisdom to look closely at our ideas and beliefs, and to check them against our experience of life. However, in traditional Buddhist terminology, this can at most only take us from wrong view to right view. Through testing our ideas against our actual experience, we produce a more accurate description of life. This process is a large step in the right direction, but it is not yet the 'wisdom beyond words' – the perfect wisdom of Mañjuśrī. To attain that we have to cease relying on concepts altogether, and take a firm stand on our direct experience of life.

Some years ago, when I was first meditating on Mañjuśrī, I used to be troubled by an unwanted image which seemed to go against the whole spirit of the practice. As I visualized Mañjuśrī's gleaming figure, holding the book to his heart and brandishing the flaming sword above his head, something would happen. With a powerful and dexterous movement, Mañjuśrī would bring down his sword, and slice it neatly through the book. This would be repeated over and over, and it bothered me as it was not 'supposed' to happen.

I subsequently came to appreciate this odd image. It was as though Mañjuśrī was assaying book after book with his razor-sharp sword of wisdom. One by one, he was taking the religious teachings and philosophies of humanity and putting them to the test. Wherever the book's author had been ensnared by words and concepts, the sword would encounter resistance, and the book would be cut into pieces.

In my mind's eye, I saw Mañjuśrī steadily working, with a mountain of neatly cut volumes of dogma and metaphysical speculation growing at his feet. I saw him patiently working on, searching, until at last he brought down his sword on a book and the sword passed clean through, leaving it intact. That volume was the Perfection of Wisdom, in which there are no concepts to hold on to, and words are used only as pointers to direct experience. As I watched, Mañjuśrī joyfully took up that volume, and he has held it to his heart ever since.

The path of spiritual swordplay

To take up a sādhana is to adopt a particular path to Enlightenment. The path of Mañjuśrī is the path of the spiritual swordsman. To follow it means taking up his fiery sword and learning to be expert at using it. It is a magic sword, more mighty than King Arthur's Excalibur. Once taken up, it cannot be sheathed until suffering has been defeated.

You have to be careful how you take it up, however. It is so sharp that a piece of the finest silk just laid across its edge will be divided cleanly in two. If you grasp it wrongly you will be cut or burned. You grasp it wrongly by misunderstanding the wisdom teachings, by taking them literally when they can never be more than 'fingers pointing to the moon'. If you become obsessed with the wisdom teachings as words, you are in a worse position than before, as you have used the medicine to add to the illness. Nāgārjuna says that it is better to have a self-view as high as Mount Meru than to have a wrong view of śūnyatā. To become obsessed with śūnyatā as though it were a state, a thing, or a sort of black hole, is to add another head to your first one, as Zen has it. Śūnyatā is just a concept to help us see through concepts, and realize that words are just clumsy tools for describing experience, and can never adequately encapsulate it.

So we have to grasp the sword of wisdom by the vajra handle of direct experience. We have to keep checking that our ideas and language are true to our experience, or as true as they can be, and not work the other way round: limiting our experience of ourselves and the world to what our ideas tell us it should be.

Having grasped the handle correctly, we can begin to wield the sword. We can use its two sharp blades to cut through the dualistic concepts we impose on our experience. Language divides the world into opposites, into dualities. The double-edged sword of wisdom cuts them down two by two: self and other, existence and non-existence, masculine and feminine, white and black, moving and stationary, heaven and hell, finite and infinite. The two flashing edges of the sword slice through subtler and subtler dualities until, at last, they meet in the fiery tip. That point where the flames dance is the point where all dualities are fused: the point where cold steel supports hot flame. It is the point where time and space disappear. It is the point where we pass through the fires of śūnyatā and experience Reality directly.

When we reach this point we shall have followed the path of Mañjuśrī to its endless end. Then we shall be Mañjuśrī, the beautiful prince, the hero of the Dharma. The sword of wisdom will be ours by right. We shall take it into battle against dualistic thinking. We shall use it to cut through the tangled knots of confusion and ignorance that fetter living beings. With its flaming point we shall burn to ashes all their suffering. We shall be invincible, for wisdom is the blow of Reality which cannot be parried.

Vajrapāṇi – wrathful form

Four

Vajrapāṇi – the Path of Heroic Transformation

What frightens you most? A few years ago I read a survey in a popular magazine in which people were asked this question. I found the answers surprising. Death came fourth. Other high scorers were spiders, snakes, and being trapped in a lift. Top of the list, though it involved no danger to life or limb, was having to speak in public. Why should so many people find the prospect of having to stand up and talk in front of their fellow human beings a fate worse than death? It can certainly be difficult to find a few well-chosen words, but why is it frightening? Why do people feel shy, embarrassed, or afraid?

As part of an audience you can blend happily into the group. But when it is your turn to get up and speak, you separate yourself from the group. You tell people what you think and feel. By implication, often, you tell them what *they* should think and feel. You are on the spot, and you really have to take responsibility for your views and opinions. You have, above all, to risk failing, or incurring the disapproval of the group. For most of us this is nerve-racking, for the road from dependence on groups and group approval to true independence is long and hard. Every step we take, however, is a step towards freedom, and an Enlightened person is not emotionally dependent on anything mundane. Enlightenment could be described as a state of complete non-dependence.

There is another aspect to the fear of giving talks in front of an audience. In this situation we may experience, more clearly and strongly than usual, the tendency to psychological projection – to experience some aspect of our psyche indirectly, projected onto someone or something around us. When we give a talk we can project our ability to look, so that we no longer really see our audience, but we are acutely aware of everyone looking at us. We can project our critical faculty: all of a sudden we have no idea whether the talk we are giving is good or bad, but we experience the audience as judging our every word. Most relevant of all, we can project our power. When we stand up to speak, we can experience the audience as more powerful than us. We feel outnumbered by 25, 50, or 1,000 to 1. Then we implode. We may feel weak, shy, fumbling, even terrified. However, if when speaking to an audience we own our own strength, we can relax. We feel full of energy. We do not feel at odds with our audience. Inspiration begins to flow. Words pour forth.

Through meditation and the practice of awareness we can learn to recognize and reassimilate psychological projections. However, the state of psychological wholeness brought about by integrating such projections is still very far short of Enlightenment. On a deeper level we shall still be projecting assumptions onto the world. For example, we project concepts of permanence onto what is really a mere flux of processes to produce a world of fixed 'things'.

Eventually, Buddhism aims to help us to see that our idea of the external world is also a projection we have built up by investing energy in it over a long period of time. The Dharma consists of methods for withdrawing the energy we invest and dissipate in the world of appearances, and concentrating it in ourselves as self-aware subjects. If we succeed in this task, then the duality of subject and object, which we have seen is the major barrier to Enlightenment, disappears. Things only appear to us as objects if we invest them with energies we do not acknowledge as our own. In reality we are whole, but we experience the world in terms of ourselves as subject, isolated from other people and objects, because we are divided against ourselves. Our energies are split.

For the purpose of everyday spiritual practice, this task of integrating energy, of making it available to us as aware individuals, can be more simply put. One of the challenges of Buddhist practice is to become less passive, to stop being victims of circumstance. More positively, this means seizing the initiative in life, becoming initiators of positive change, and working to mould everything into more perfect forms. This applies both to mental states and to what appears to us as the external world. Moulding our existence in this way does not mean crudely using power. We only use force against what we do not recognize or acknowledge as our own.

One of the best symbols in Buddhism for this process of rallying energy, seizing the initiative, overcoming dependence on externals, and attaining a concentrated and free flow of energy, is Vajrapāṇi (holder of the diamond thunderbolt, Tibetan *Chakna Dorje*), the embodiment of spiritual energy and power. He takes the initiative in ceaselessly working for the good of all sentient beings. He embodies spiritual heroism, daring to face our own projected power, re-own it, and place it at the service of the Dharma.

The path of Vajrapāṇi

One picture is worth a thousand words, so let us see how this heroic figure appears. Like all Buddhas and Bodhisattvas, his nature is the freedom of śūnyatā, so he appears in the midst of empty space. He is royal blue in colour, sitting on a moon mat that rests on a royal-blue lotus throne. He is seated in the posture of royal ease, his left hand resting on the moon mat. He is dressed in silks and precious jewels, and is young, handsome, and smiling. On the palm of his right hand, standing upright, perfectly balanced, is a golden vajra. In his heart is the deep-blue seed syllable *hūṃ*. His body radiates vibrant energy and power. This is a peaceful form of Vajrapāṇi. (Those of you who are familiar with another of his common forms may have been expecting a rather different kind of figure. He will appear a little later. You may already be able to hear his footsteps approaching from several world-systems away.)

Vajrapāṇi is the chief Bodhisattva, the family protector, of the Vajra family. Thus he is associated with the blue Buddha Akṣobhya, with transcendental wisdom, and with the power, strength, and untiring energy of the elephant.

Vajrapāṇi is sometimes also referred to as Guhyapati. This is translated by Herbert Guenther as 'lord of the mystic teaching'. *Guhya* means secret, so he could be called 'lord of secrets'. The Vajrayāna, or Tantric path, is also known as the path of *guhyamantra* (secret mantra).

Vajrapāṇi is a figure who goes through a most interesting process of development in Buddhist literature and practice. He appears in the Pali suttas as a kind of protective spirit or daemon of Śākyamuni Buddha. For example, in the *Ambaṭṭha Suttanta* of the Pali canon[22] a young brahmin, called Ambaṭṭha, puffed up with his own learning and caste prejudice, goes to see the Buddha. In the course of their meeting he repeatedly insults the Buddha, saying that the Śākya clan from which he derives are menials who should pay homage to the brahmins. The Buddha then tells the story of the nobility of his clan and puts to Ambaṭṭha an embarrassing question: 'Is it not true that you are descended from a Śākya slave girl?' Ambaṭṭha avoids answering, and the Buddha repeats his question. For the second time Ambaṭṭha keeps silent, at which the Buddha gives him a curious warning. 'You had better answer, now, Ambaṭṭha. This is no time for you to hold your peace. For whosoever, Ambaṭṭha, does not, even up to the third time of asking, answer a reasonable question put by a Tathāgata, his head splits into pieces on the spot.'

Looking up, Ambaṭṭha is startled to see, above the Buddha's head, Vajirapāṇi (the Pali form; Vajrapāṇi is Sanskrit), holding a glowing, fiery thunderbolt, poised and ready to dash his head to pieces. Terrified, he acknowledges that what the Buddha says about his ancestry is true. The commentator Buddhaghosa identifies this Vajirapāṇi with the god Indra, who among his other manifestations is the god of storm, depicted holding a thunderbolt, and is known as Vajri, the thunderer.

In early Buddhist scriptures, Indra, the great Indian god of Vedic times, is shown in attendance on the Buddha. However, as time passes, Indra becomes less important for Buddhism (and for Hinduism) and Vajrapāṇi's stature grows. In early Buddhist texts, Vajrapāṇi is a *yakṣa*, a local deity,[23] who functions as a kind of guardian spirit of the Buddha. In early Mahāyāna sūtras he still has this role. For example, in the *Sūtra of Golden Light* he is referred to as 'great general of the yakṣas'. By the time of the early Tantric texts he has become a more central character. In the *Mañjuśrī Mūla Kalpa* he is the main representative of the Vajra family, and is one of the two main attendants on Śākyamuni in the mandala, where he is surrounded by an entourage of four goddesses. In a later Tantra, the *Tattvasaṃgraha*, he is the predominant figure.

In this way, Vajrapāṇi proceeds from being the leader of the yakṣas to a Great Bodhisattva. However, his development does not end there. Being associated with the vajra, the symbol which gave its name to the specifically Tantric form of Buddhism, the Vajrayāna, in some Tantras he is regarded as chief among Bodhisattvas, and finally, as Vajradhara (bearer of the thunderbolt), he becomes an expression of Buddhahood itself. In later Tantric tradition, as received by the Tibetans, Vajradhara and Vajrapāṇi come to be distinguished iconographically, but at this earlier stage there is no such distinction and Vajrapāṇi is frequently referred to as a Buddha. In China and Japan Vajrapāṇi is known just as Vajra (Japanese *Kongo*), and he plays a significant role in Shingon – the Tantric Buddhism of Japan.

In a popular Mahāyāna legend, the Buddhas meet together on top of Mount Meru to work out how to gain the elixir of life (*amṛta*) – the only antidote to a poison with which demons are afflicting mankind. Through churning the ocean with Mount Meru *amṛta* comes to the surface. The *amṛta* is entrusted to Vajrapāṇi. He leaves it unguarded for a moment and it is stolen by Rāhu. Vajrapāṇi fights him and wins back the *amṛta*, but it is defiled. The Buddhas make Vajrapāṇi drink the defiled *amṛta*, and his body turns a dark blue from the poison.

This story is similar to the Hindu legend which tells of the gods churning the sea of milk with Mount Mandara and the snake Vasuki. The snake gave forth venom which fell down in a great stream, threatening all living beings. Shiva came to the rescue by drinking the poison, and as a result his neck turned blue. One of the names by which Shiva is known is Nilakantha (blue throat).

As the Bodhisattva of power or energy, Vajrapāṇi is obviously intimately connected with the Vajrayāna because the Vajrayāna sees everything in terms of energy. The vajra itself, the diamond thunderbolt, which Vajrapāṇi holds, is unstoppable and unbreakable. This is perhaps because it is made of pure energy.

The path of Vajrapāṇi, then, is very much concerned with seeing the entire universe as consisting of energy, and rallying that energy to the cause of spiritual development. Through practice of his sādhana your mind becomes like pure vajra – like a diamond that cuts without being cut. You learn to seize the spiritual initiative, and affect the world positively without allowing it to have any negative effect on you.

Vajrapāṇi is a heroic figure. His path is one of overcoming fear. To walk this path we have to confront everything that terrifies us. Often what is really most frightening for us as human beings is our unowned power, the energy we could possess. A few years ago, on my way to lead a three-month meditation retreat in Italy, I stopped off in Chamonix, at the foot of the Alps. A few hours later, a friend and I were in a cable car, hanging by a thread above the valley thousands of feet below. Off to our left was the massive bulk of Mont Blanc. Gazing across at it I realized that I found it very beautiful, but also terrible, awe-inspiring, and frightening. Exploring my feelings further, I saw that it was not the peaceful rock of the mountain that was affecting me. Faced with this external vastness, an intuition was being sparked off within me. I understood that, enthralled by the mountain, it was the sheer volume of my own potential energy that I was experiencing.

When I looked down through space to the miniature houses below, I felt a surge of energy. At the same time I could feel myself struggling to prevent something from becoming conscious. Suddenly I knew what it was that I had been trying to exclude from my awareness – it was a vision of sheer freedom, of becoming someone prepared to plunge into the vast abyss of Liberation.

The prospect of walking the path of Vajrapāṇi – confronting our own energy, power, and freedom – can be terrifying. To experience the sheer exultant bliss of success on this path would be awesome. We should lose our heads: our safe, conventional judgements. We should lose our average, comfortable selves. We should break cover and emerge from our quiet anonymity in the group. We should no longer masquerade as innocent bystanders in life, we should be the main actors. We should begin to expand, to swell with tremendous energies. Where would it end?

Bodhisattvas as states of mind

Before we try to imagine where it would end, we need to look more deeply at the question of what a Buddha or Bodhisattva is. We can see a Buddha or Bodhisattva figure as being 'out there' or 'in here'. As the distinction between subject and object is illusory, one view cannot be more true than the other. It can be useful to think of transcendental figures as being outside us, since we then recognize that they are beyond anything that we currently experience.

Although it can be quite legitimate, at least in the earlier stages of spiritual practice, to think of Buddhas and Bodhisattvas as being external to ourselves, and to try to get in touch with them, there is also a danger. That danger is of being too literal-minded. If we take the figures too literally, they cease to become embodiments of our potential and become distant, beautiful figures whom we are content to worship from afar. If this happens, there is little difference between a distant Bodhisattva on a lotus throne and an old man with a white beard sitting on a cloud. It is no use projecting all the power and beauty of our own minds onto a Bodhisattva and then admiring it, if the net result is that we feel as weak and helpless as before.

So while, perhaps, for certain purposes, we may see Vajrapāṇi outside ourselves, we need also to recognize that he is a symbol of a mental state. Being a transcendental figure, he represents a way in which we can permanently reorganize our being. Visualizing a Bodhisattva is a way of giving us a feeling for what it would be like to reorganize our mental state in an Enlightened way.

Now we can return to our question: what would we experience were we to follow Vajrapāṇi's heroic path to Enlightenment? If we just carried on confronting fear and releasing energy indefinitely, how would our minds feel when we reached the end of that path, when there was no fear left, and all our energies were liberated? How could we convey that wild freedom?

Sometimes we would feel very peaceful and calm, like the radiant royal-blue figure of the peaceful Vajrapāṇi. At other times, though, we could be seized with a surfeit of energy. We might feel more like a bull in the china shop of saṃsāra, smashing illusions and self-deceptions with a great crashing sound.

We would be standing alone like a mythic hero, or great warrior – a champion of the Dharma. We would be engaged in an exultant spiritual battle, on the side of all living beings against the forces of suffering. At times we might be an embodiment of spiritual impatience, urging people that now is the time to break out of saṃsāra, now is the time to put Māra to flight, now is the time to stamp out craving and hatred – to jump up and down on them until they beg for mercy – now is the time to dance on the grave of ignorance. We should feel ecstatic, victorious, having seen that our enemies – craving, hatred, and ignorance – were all just paper tigers. We had routed them.

This would be our experience. However, perhaps even this description does not do that state justice. Perhaps the best way of describing that experience, that state of mind, would be to say that we had become the *wrathful* form of Vajrapāṇi.

Colossal, deep blue, body swelling with unquenchable energy, we fill the universe. We are stamping to the right, standing on a huge sun disc supported by a lotus throne, wearing a tiger skin around our loins. A great garland of human skulls hangs from our neck. Wreathed with snakes, and with a diadem of five skulls, we stand unshakeable. Our left hand makes the gesture of warding off demons and enemies of the Dharma. Our right hand is raised aloft, brandishing a golden vajra, prepared to hurl it. The vajra is the infallible weapon, which never misses, always destroys its target, and then returns to our hand. Our body is surrounded by an aureole of crackling flames. Our great shout of *hūṃ* echoes across the universe, a battle cry and joyful shout of victory.

This wrathful form of Vajrapāṇi does not appear in the Mahāyāna texts, which focus on the compassionate nature of the Bodhisattvas. He is a product of Tantra. With this figure, his energies totally aroused, wild and free, the Tantra tries to convey to us the experience of the heroic, fearless qualities of the Enlightened mind.

As with all other Buddha and Bodhisattva figures, though, Vajrapāṇi is not just a symbol for the conclusion of the path. Visualizing him is a way of following that path and moving closer to the goal. (This language of 'path' and 'goal' is not very satisfactory. As Enlightenment is not a 'finishing line' – a point at which you stop developing – you cannot really talk of a 'final goal'. The 'goal' of the spiritual life is to be absolutely on the path, to be totally engaged in the process of spiritual development.)

Through visualizing Vajrapāṇi's form and reciting his mantra: *oṃ vajrapāṇi hūṃ*, we absorb something of his Enlightened qualities. Through setting our minds concentratedly on an embodiment of such energy and spiritual power, we gradually begin to contact our own strength and heroism. Through dwelling on the goal we become increasingly identified with it.

Vajrapāṇi as the experience of breakthrough

Whether or not we take up his sādhana, we need Vajrapāṇi's qualities in our spiritual practice. Without energy and heroism we shall never break through the obstacles that stand between us and Buddhahood. This is something else that Vajrapāṇi symbolizes: ecstatic breaking through to higher levels of consciousness. The usual pattern in spiritual practice, for most people, is to go for a period of time without anything major appearing to happen. Then there is a breakthrough – something dramatic happens, which shows us clearly that we are changing, that a new and more positive element is entering into the mandala of our spiritual life.

Some people's development is more tempestuous than others'. The Zen master Hakuin, for instance, experienced a tumultuous spiritual life, with many major and minor breakthroughs and insight experiences. For others, Enlightenment matures more gently, like fruit gradually ripening until it falls. These things seem to depend on one's temperament, mode of practice, and the amount of energy one puts into changing oneself.

Nonetheless, the general pattern is for there to be a quiet build-up of energy and then a breakthrough, just as water builds up silently against a dyke until there is a crack and it pours through. Sometimes people are overly concerned with achieving breakthroughs, and fail to acknowledge the effects of quiet, continuing practice. Then spiritual teachers have to resort to telling stories like that of the man who was trying to split a great rock, and only succeeded at the twentieth blow. The other nineteen blows did not appear to achieve anything, but they set up the conditions for the breakthrough. You cannot start with the twentieth blow.

Vajrapāṇi, then, symbolizes the experience of breaking through, especially breaking through to insight into Reality. His wrathful form represents the tremendous amount of energy required to achieve that breakthrough. It also graphically illustrates the energy that is liberated when that breakthrough is achieved. To bring about that radical transformation, to reorganize our minds to transcend suffering, we have to destroy whatever stands in our way. Traditionally there are said to be three things that hold us back from achieving insight. These are (1) belief in a fixed unchanging self, (2) sceptical doubt, and (3) attachment to rites and rituals as ends in themselves. These three limiting patterns all have to be broken through.[24]

But for most of us insight into Reality may still be some way off. More immediately, perhaps we can think of breaking through in two areas. These also require a degree of heroism to develop, but they are quite attainable by anyone who is prepared to risk being themselves.

The first is breaking through to real communication. This releases a tremendous amount of energy. To be able to be fully yourself with at least one or two other people, to break out of isolation to a true meeting with them, is an essential human experience, and forms the basis most people need for their higher, spiritual development. However, really communicating with other people can feel like a risky business. As with speaking in front of a group, we have to take responsibility for who we are, for what we really think and feel. It will be much easier for us to do this if we are in touch with a sangha, a spiritual community where open communication and the development of friendship are acknowledged as goals towards which everyone is striving.

Getting closer to other people involves running two risks. When we hold ourselves at a distance we usually keep our feelings of attraction and aversion for people at a low level. As we come closer, as our communication deepens, both these feelings come to the fore. We may have to acknowledge attraction in the form of sexual feelings, or aversion in the form of anger or resentment. It is at the point that they become aware of these feelings that people often back away from communication. However, these strong feelings are just the dragons that guard the treasure of intimate communication and deep friendship. If your movement towards other people is based on real friendliness, these other feelings can be put into perspective, and you can increasingly find that you are developing with other people *kalyāṇa mitratā* – 'spiritual friendship' – which the Buddha once declared to be 'the whole of the spiritual life'.[25]

Our second breakthrough can be into confidence. Lack of confidence is one of the greatest limiting factors on many people's spiritual practice. They have confidence in the Three Jewels: the Buddha, Dharma, and Sangha. They accept that they work to help vast numbers of people to develop. Yet somehow they do not believe that Buddhism will really work for them, that they can really transform themselves. Underlying all their seeming efforts to practise is the word 'but'. Some people lack confidence through feelings of unworthiness and existential guilt. Whatever the reason, these feelings have to go, to be replaced by confidence both in the Three Jewels and in themselves.

Lack of confidence in oneself can be overcome by reflecting on the Dharma, and how through its faithful practice ordinary men and women have transformed themselves. The encouragement of spiritual friends can be a great source of strength, as can the practice of Maitrī Bhāvanā – a meditation on loving-kindness – paying particular attention to oneself. In the West, many people lack confidence because they set themselves unrealistically high standards and then fear that they will not live up to them. So it is important in the early stages of Dharma practice not to overburden yourself by expecting too much too soon. Rather than expecting yourself to be highly creative, it is enough to start thinking in terms of being useful and productive – just getting your energies moving. Rather than giving yourself a hard time if your meditation is not deep and blissful, it is enough to be satisfied that you are making an effort to work on your mental states. In this way you undermine the attitudes that stop you from trying, that stop you getting on with your practice. Once you allow yourself to try, once you are practising the Dharma, you will gradually begin to notice changes and developments, and confidence will naturally arise.

Breaking through to confidence involves developing a feeling that our lives are potent, by smashing through limiting views of ourselves as useless or weak. Vajrapāṇi's path is one of activity, of taking the risk of trying to change, not of sitting back and grumbling about how things are.

Seizing the vajra

Vajrapāṇi offers us the prospect of seizing the vajra, of entering the spiritual battleground as a warrior. Through his wisdom we have the chance to see that our fate is in our own hands. The ten fetters which hold us back from Enlightenment are not external, nor even rogue forces in our own minds. They are simply characteristic ways in which we organize our consciousness. They are habitual ways in which we use our minds to fetter ourselves.

Vajrapāṇi's wisdom helps us to see that all our fears and hesitations, all the monsters and bogymen with which we hold ourselves back from happiness, are just our energies misdirected. They are all products of our own mind – and we can work on our minds to reorganize it, to channel our energies in ever more satisfying directions.

With these realizations we can seize the vajra. We can begin to take total responsibility for our lives, to take the initiative, to reorient and transform our minds, until it feels charged with tremendous energy. If we continue making this effort, then finally the mind will feel like a vast blue sky, with an enormous source of spiritual vitality and heroism standing triumphant in its midst.

Green Tārā

Five

Green Tārā – the Quick Way to Wisdom

In the previous chapter, on Vajrapāṇi, we looked at the various negative mental habits that have to be broken through for transcendental insight to arise. This insight is experienced as beyond time and space, so Buddhist teachers hold the view (as do some Western philosophers) that time is a function of consciousness. So let us step outside time, at least in imagination, into the boundless blue sky of the Timeless....

In the pristine blue sky is a huge white cloud. The cloud is made of light, as is everything in this inner space. Just by looking at it, we are filled with serenity. It somehow radiates kindness.

In the middle of that great white light is a pair of blue eyes, gazing downwards. They are the most beautiful eyes the world has ever seen. As we look into those sapphire eyes we see scenes reflected in them. We see women painfully giving birth to new generations of hope, and after a little space those hopes lying, helpless as the day they were born, on their deathbeds. Reflected across those eyes, armies march in pomp and pageantry, and retreat back across them in tattered ranks, carrying their wounded and dying. There are men dressed in skins carrying clubs, men in chain mail brandishing swords, men in khaki bearing rifles, technicians in casual clothes looking at screens and pressing buttons. There are mud huts and great cities. There are lovers together, lovers separated, lovers who hate each other. The reflections go on forever. The scenes are not just of human beings, but also of animals and other forms of life. The reflections never stop. The more we watch, the more repetitive they seem to be. The faces change, the landscapes vary, but there is always birth, building, new hope, a brief flowering,... then weakening, undermining, destruction – old age, sickness, death.

The reflections become unclear, like images mirrored in a troubled lake. Tears form like dew in the exquisite eyes, and fall in two great streams. They fall to earth, where they form a pool. They pour down endlessly in response to the sufferings mirrored in the tear-filled eyes. Gradually, a great lake of tears forms. The waters in the centre of the lake are ruffled by something slowly emerging from their depths. Out of the lake of tears rises a pastel-blue lotus flower of an extraordinary delicacy. A stream of tears falls into the soft heart of the lotus and transforms it into a white full-moon disc.

Slowly, just above the surface of the moon disc, jade-green light appears. Its outlines become more definite, without gaining any solidity. We are watching the birth of a princess, a goddess, a Bodhisattva.

She is jade green in colour, clad in a rainbow skirt, with a meditation sash tied around her body. She is decked in precious jewels: bracelets, armlets, anklets, necklaces, earrings, and a tiara of gems. She is seated, her left foot resting on her right thigh in meditation posture. Her right foot steps gracefully down, and as it does so a small pastel-blue lotus and moon mat rise out of the lake to make a footrest. Her right arm reaches down, the back of her hand resting on her right knee. Her palm is open in a mudrā of supreme giving. Her left hand is held in front of her heart, palm outwards, the thumb and ring finger together, so that the other three fingers point upwards. This mudrā bestows protection and fearlessness through invoking the Three Jewels. Her thumb and ring finger delicately grasp the stem of a lotus flower, which curves upwards to open into a spray of blossoms by her left shoulder. There is a bud, a half-opened flower, and a fully opened blossom of pale blue. She is sixteen years old, full-breasted, with flowing black hair. She is supremely beautiful.

Her apparitional birth complete, her jade eyelids open for the first time, to reveal two perfect blue eyes, identical to those from which she was born. She looks out over the world and the lake of tears, and upward to the white cloud of compassion far above her, and her face breaks into a smile of such beauty and tenderness that the whole world trembles with joy.

From her heart, rays of light begin to pour forth. Shining through the rain of compassionate tears still falling around her they produce myriad rainbows, arcing and dancing in all directions. Every rainbow whispers a sound. They carry it like aery messengers out from her heart. They whisper the sound to the troubled waters of the lake, which become soothed and still. They whisper it to the falling teardrops, which reverse their direction and turn into precious offerings to the cloud of compassion high above them. The rainbows whisper the sound to the universe, to you and me. The sound is *oṃ tāre tuttāre ture svāhā*. It is the mantra of the beautiful green princess. It is the beginning of the end of all our suffering.

We have been witnessing the birth of the Bodhisattva Tārā. Tradition has it that she was born from the tears of Avalokiteśvara, the Bodhisattva of Compassion, as he contemplated the sufferings of the universe.[26] Being born from Avalokiteśvara's tears, she is sometimes referred to as the 'quintessence of compassion'. She is compassion at its most gentle and heartfelt.

Encountering Tārā's beautiful figure, we are also, perhaps, experiencing Enlightenment in its most accessible form. Tārā is very approachable. The lotus on which she sits grows out of a pool on the earth. However, when we speak of Enlightenment in its most accessible form, this has to be taken poetically. In a sense, because there is an absolute discontinuity between the mundane and the transcendental paths, you cannot speak of getting closer to Enlightenment. However, you can say that in some situations the conditions are better than in others for making that distanceless leap from the conditioned to the Unconditioned. This idea is fully worked out in the doctrine of Buddha seeds, which gained currency in Chinese Buddhism. According to this teaching, each of the six realms of existence, with their characteristic mental states, vary in their potential as launching pads from which to gain Buddhahood. One way of understanding a visualization sādhana is to know that through practising it you enter a new world. You create a realm from which it is as easy as possible to gain Enlightenment. Tārā's beautiful realm, which you enter through practising her sādhana, is packed full of Buddha seeds.

Tārā is Enlightenment stepping down to us, reaching out a hand to lift us up. She is the Voidness clothed in its finest raiment. However, her accessibility can cause misunderstandings. Because she is Enlightenment presenting itself to us in such a familiar and attractive disguise, we can easily fail to see her true nature. For men she may function as an anima figure, for women as a role model, and for both sexes as a form of earth or nature goddess. However, she is not defined by any of these views, and finally she is none of, and more than, any of them. She is the embodiment of transcendental compassion. She is the inconceivable, the unknowable, the ungraspable, presenting itself to us in a way that is easy for us poor mortals to relate to. This is made clear by the fact that her whole body is vacuous, made of light, appearing yet empty, neither existent nor non-existent.

As we see more deeply into her nature, we come to understand that she is not green, does not hold a lotus, does not reach down with her right leg. Her beautiful form is just the gateway to a deep inner experience that has neither colour, nor form, nor sex. The external appearance of Tārā is just a molehill hiding a mountain of Enlightened qualities. So Tārā is both easily approachable and fathomless, familiar yet beyond understanding.

Tārā in Buddhist tradition

Tārā belongs to two Buddha families at once (perhaps because she is so beautiful that everyone wants to claim her for their own). She is the green consort of Amoghasiddhi. (The five Buddhas are often depicted with female consorts in Tantric sādhanas.) Yet she is born from Avalokiteśvara's tears, and hence is a product of the Lotus family. In *thangkas* and sādhanas she may appear with either Amoghasiddhi or Amitābha above her head.

Her name can mean 'star', but it is usually understood to mean 'saviouress', or 'one who ferries across' from saṃsāra to nirvāṇa. In Tibet she is known as Dolma or Drolma. Her history can be traced in such books as Stephan Beyer's *The Cult of Tārā*. (One of the advantages of being a Tārā devotee is that there is probably more written about her in Western languages than about any other Buddha or Bodhisattva figure.)

Plate One Vajrapāṇi – wrathful form

Plate Two Green Tārā

Plate Three White Tārā

Plate Four Maitreya

Plate Five Prajñāpāramitā

Plate Six Vajrasattva

Plate Seven Padmasambhava with the set of eight manifestations

Plate Eight Milarepa

The attention paid to Tārā by Western scholars reflects the tremendous devotion shown her by Tibetans. In Indian Buddhism, too, she gathered enough of a following to appear in many different forms. The Green Tārā is the most commonly represented and meditated upon, though there are many sādhanas of the White Tārā, associated with long life, whom we shall meet in the next chapter. There is also a very important set of twenty-one Tārās who are frequently depicted in Tibetan *thangkas*, usually with the Green Tārā occupying a central position.

Tārā appears in Buddhist canonical literature only at the point where the Mahāyāna is beginning to show Tantric influence. Although she is an embodiment of Avalokiteśvara's compassion, she does not appear in those early Mahāyāna sūtras in which he plays a central part. The text that has come down to us which provides the basis for many later Tārā sādhanas is an Indian Tantric compilation known as *The Origin of All Rites of Tārā, Mother of All the Tathāgatas*, which was translated into Tibetan in the late twelfth century.[27]

Chapter 3 of that work includes the 'Homages to the Twenty-One Tārās', which Martin Willson says 'became in Tibet the most popular of all hymns to Tārā, or indeed to any deity. Still today, at Tibetan monasteries around the world, it is chanted several times daily by all the monks, and on special occasions and when it is desired to enlist the Venerable Mother's aid for some particular purpose it is this praise that is recited over and over again by both monks and laity, and in some cases by nuns too.'[28] Repetition of the 'Homages' also forms a central part of the very common devotional ritual known as the four mandala offering to Tārā. Here, the word *mandala* is used in a different sense from the mandala of the five Buddhas. It refers to a visualization of the entire universe, along with everything beautiful and valuable, which is repeatedly offered to Tārā in the course of the ritual.

In Tibetan history, one name stands out above all others in connection with Tārā, and that is Atīśa. Atīśa was a great Indian scholar, who answered an invitation to go to Tibet in the eleventh century, despite a prediction that the journey would shorten his life by twenty years. Atīśa is a central figure for Tibetan Buddhism. His 'Lamp for the Path' is a model for the Lam Rim or 'Graduated Path' teachings. He introduced some much needed reforms into the Buddhism of Tibet, and founded the Kadam school, whose adherents were the spiritual ancestors of the Gelukpas. Above all, though, Atīśa had the deepest love and devotion for the Bodhicitta teachings and for Tārā. This communicated itself to everyone he met. It is from the crystal spring of his own practice that so much of the devotion to Tārā in Tibet flowed.

Incidentally, Atīśa is the author of a remark which is as telling for Westerners today as it was for Tibetans 900 years ago. 'The Tibetans', he said, 'practise a hundred deities without achieving one, whereas the ancient Indian masters practised one, and achieved a hundred.' For us Westerners, too, it is important to learn the crucial lesson of fidelity in spiritual practice. Let loose in the transcendental sweet-shop of the Mahāyāna and Vajrayāna, it is easy to start nibbling here and there, getting bored and moving on, without ever fully savouring one practice and letting it nourish us. So while various practices can be used for specific purposes, it is crucial that we have one figure at the centre of our mandala to whom we really give our hearts. Tārā is a particularly easy figure to open ourselves to in this way.

The green form of Tārā is especially associated with fearlessness and spontaneous helpfulness. Like a mother instantly and unthinkingly leaping into danger if her child is threatened, Green Tārā steps down at once to give aid and protection to any living being who calls on her. This function as protectress extends, in popular Buddhist tradition, far beyond the spiritual realm. Many Tārā devotees would call on her or recite her mantra to guard against mundane perils and difficulties as well. For example, Tārā is said to protect one from the 'eight great terrors': lions, elephants, fire, snakes, robbers, captivity, shipwreck, and demons. Sometimes this list is understood symbolically, as relating to the spiritual dangers of pride, delusion, anger, envy, wrong views, avarice, attachment, and doubt, respectively. However, many people take the idea quite literally, and there is a wealth of Indian and Tibetan stories to attest to the magical way in which, through calling on Tārā, people have escaped extreme physical danger. Because of her protective powers, Tārā was especially popular with merchants and traders, who often ran great risks on their journeys. Perhaps some of the rapid spread of devotion to Tārā can be explained by the fact that such people, who had learned to call upon her in times of danger, became in effect her travelling emissaries.

Traditionally, Tārā is compared to a virgin, a mother, and a queen. She is like a virgin inasmuch as she is completely pure. She is unstained by the mundane. Her morality is unblemished. On a metaphysical level, too, she is pure. Her wisdom is as eternally fresh as the pastel sky-lotus on which she sits. Arising out of the Voidness she is pure of any conception of inherent existence. Virginity and chastity are also symbols of wholeness and independence. Tārā is spiritually complete in herself. The experience of her wisdom and compassion needs no addition or complement.

As we have seen, she has a mother's compassion and instant response to suffering. She cares for all beings as though each were her only child. Like a mother, she is very accepting. Here we come to the interesting question of the way in which Buddhas and Bodhisattvas have different 'characters'. From deep experience of practising their sādhanas, and comparing notes, Buddhist meditators have built up 'profiles' of the various deities. Some deities, it seems, are more exacting than others. There are those whom it would be wise not to displease by forgetting to perform their sādhana.

Once again, we can interpret this in 'internal' or 'external' terms. We can either say that different figures 'have' certain qualities, or we can say that sādhanas differ in the kind of impact they have on the psychophysical energies of the meditator. As these effects are usually attributed to the figure visualized, in this case we shall use 'external' language and talk about Tārā's character being very accepting.

So it is said that if you are very tired one morning and get up too late to perform more than an abbreviated version of her sādhana, Tārā doesn't mind. She is always understanding and forgiving. (Perhaps even if you write about her, and fail to do justice to her beauty, she will understand. Let us hope she will find a way to communicate something of herself anyhow.)

Lastly, Tārā is like a queen. She exercises spiritual sovereignty. She is dignified and fearless. She takes responsibility for the whole universe, and lays down the law of the Dharma, to bring an end to suffering in all six realms.

We have seen Tārā's birth from Avalokiteśvara's tears. According to another legend she was of royal descent. This story is told in *The Golden Rosary, A History Illuminating the Origin of the Tantra of Tārā* by Tārānātha, a scholar of the Jonang school of Tibetan Buddhism. An immeasurable period of time ago, in a world-system called Manifold Light, lived a princess whose name was Moon of Knowledge. She was devoted to the Buddha of that world called Dundubhīśvara (Lord of the Drum). She made vast offerings to that Buddha and his retinue, and finally developed the Bodhicitta.

Then some monks urged her to pray to be reborn in a male body to follow her career as a Bodhisattva. However, the princess saw that male and female were both concepts imputed onto experience, having no existence in reality. She made a great vow, saying, 'There are many who desire Enlightenment in a man's body, but none who work for the benefit of sentient beings in the body of a woman. Therefore, until saṃsāra is empty, I shall work for the benefit of sentient beings in a woman's body.'[29]

She then stayed in her palace, practising meditation until she perfected a samādhi called 'saving all sentient beings'. By entering into this unimaginably powerful state of concentration, every morning and evening she rescued a million million sentient beings from saṃsāra. As a result, she became known as Tārā, the Saviouress.

Tārā as the quick way to wisdom

A piece of Buddhist lore about Tārā which we have not yet examined states that her sādhana is 'the quick way to wisdom'. Through her practice, insight into Reality can be easily and swiftly attained. At first sight this seems paradoxical. Tārā, after all, is the quintessence of compassion. So why should she, of all the Bodhisattvas, be regarded as the bestower of rapid insight?

Clearly, no practice can be the shortest path for everybody. The Buddha or Bodhisattva who will lead you most quickly to Enlightenment will usually be one whom you personally find inspiring. By and large, you will be best off devoting yourself to a sādhana that you really enjoy, that you feel for, that you practise wholeheartedly, of which you cannot get enough. This will serve you better than a perhaps more 'advanced' and esoteric sādhana of a figure with whom you have no emotional connection, and whose significance you may not fully understand.

That said, many people have found Tārā's practice a very quick vehicle for arriving at insight. This becomes easier to understand if we realize that insight is not an achievement of the rational mind. It is the product of the whole man, or woman, wholly attending. We have to unite head and heart, thought and feeling, into one faculty, and use that to pierce through the veil of wrong ideas and confused emotions to a direct encounter with things as they are. So gaining insight has as much to do with opening the heart as with developing the intellect. Chatrul Rimpoche, a contemporary Nyingma meditation teacher from eastern Tibet, says that 'all the great pandits [i.e. scholars] of India had Tārā for their yidam.'

One of Tārā's special attributes is the speed with which she acts. A famous song of praise to her begins, 'Homage Tārā, quick one, heroine.' She moves rapidly to help you to escape from saṃsāra, and it is wisdom which allows you to do this, so that is what she quickly bestows.

One of the reasons her practice is so effective is that she is such an intensely beautiful figure. This means that you want to contemplate her. With practice in visualization it becomes even more enjoyable to dwell on her figure than on a painting by some great artist. The more you become entranced by her beauty, the more time you will spend contemplating her. The longer you spend with her, the more her message of loving care for all that lives will communicate itself to you. 'What you set your heart upon, that you become,' according to Buddhism. Spellbound by Tārā, lost in her loveliness, you become steadily more Tārā-like. You come closer to compassion, and with that you move steadily towards wisdom.

A Green Tārā sādhana

To finish this chapter, we shall look briefly at a Tārā sādhana.[30] As with all these practices, one should first obtain permission from a qualified spiritual teacher before embarking upon it. However, this permission can sometimes come in unexpected ways. The story of how I came to take up the Tārā practice demonstrates how permission and initiation need not always be matters of formal ritual.

In my early days of visualization practice I was working on a Padmasambhava sādhana. One summer, I attended a question-and-answer session about visualization with a Buddhist teacher. He discussed the use of visualizations which would be complementary to one's main sādhana. For example, if you had been visualizing Avalokiteśvara you might take up meditation on Mañjuśrī, to balance compassion with wisdom. I thought at the time that I did not want another practice. I felt I needed a few aeons of deepening the Padmasambhava practice first. I returned to Brighton, where I was living, and thought no more about it.

A few days later I had a dream. I found myself in a queue of people all waiting to receive an initiation. It was midnight, and we were standing in a large, empty area like a car park. People disappeared one by one, until I was left alone. There was nobody in sight, and I was unsure where I should go. All I could see was a single-decker green bus, standing in a corner.

I went to it and walked up the steps. In the driver's seat was Peter, a friend of mine who was a house-painter. But though he looked just like Peter, I knew that the figure behind the wheel was actually a very accomplished Tibetan lama, on a visit to the West.

I introduced myself, explaining that I was a member of the Western Buddhist Order, and had been doing the Padmasambhava sādhana. He looked very pleased to find a Westerner seriously practising the Dharma. I said I had come for another practice. He reached down beside his steering wheel, and produced a clipboard, such as ticket inspectors use. He handed it to me, saying, 'Choose one of these.' I looked at it. It was a list of spiritual practices, mainly Tantric sādhanas, though there was one in Chinese that I did not recognize, and two in Latin, which looked as though they were parts of the Roman Catholic Mass. 'I can't quite decide,' I said after some thought, 'between Mañjuśrī and Green Tārā. But I think I'd like to ask for Green Tārā.'

His face lit up, and he said he was always especially happy to pass on that practice, as he himself had done it for many years. Then he talked of the benefits of doing it, and how beautiful it was. Finally he said, 'Right, I'll give you the initiation now.'

He closed his fist, extended his first finger, and began pointing it at my forehead. He kept moving it around the area where the psychic centre (or 'third eye') is said to be, obviously trying to find exactly the right location. As he did so I could feel panic rising inside me. Something awesome was going to happen. He was going to blow my brains out with his finger! I wanted to turn and run.

Then a voice inside me said, 'This is an initiation. You just have to relax and accept whatever happens.' As soon as I thought that, and began to relax, he said, 'Ah, that's the spot.' Then everything went black, and I seemed to lose consciousness.

I do not know how long this state lasted, and anyway time sense is different in dreams. After a period I began to revive. His face swam back into view. Just when I could see him clearly again, he began repeating the Tārā mantra. He recited it three times, and each time I repeated it after him.

Then the dream began to draw to a close. I started drifting slowly up into consciousness. All the time I could hear the soft lilt of the mantra, and I was incredibly happy and relaxed. I felt as I sometimes used to feel as a child, waking up to a summer Saturday with sunlight streaming through the window. Just before I was fully awake and about to start thinking, a voice said, 'It's all right to use the mantra now. You've had the initiation.'

I shall just mention two strange things connected with this dream. If you had asked me the previous day to take up another practice, I would have refused. If you had insisted, then, of all the figures mentioned in this series of books, Tārā was the last I would have chosen. I had no feeling for her at all. (I should perhaps say that even after this dream I did not think it appropriate just to start practising a Tārā sādhana. It was only after relating the dream to my teacher, talking it over, and receiving permission from him that I began meditating on Tārā.) Secondly, a year or so later, Peter became a member of the Western Buddhist Order called

Jyotipala ('protector of the light'). Without any prompting from me, he took up the Green Tārā practice.

There must be hundreds of Green Tārā sādhanas. They range from some quite brief evocations to be found in the Lower Tantras to the fairly complex practices associated with Cittamani (jewel of the mind) Tārā, the Highest Tantra form of the goddess. The meditation we are going to look at is a simple one, which falls into three stages.

1 Becoming Tārā

At the start of the practice we dissolve everyday appearances into the voidness of the blue sky. Then in our heart appears a pale-blue lotus flower, on top of which is a white moon mat. Standing on the moon mat is the letter *tāṃ*, made of jade green or turquoise light. Next we appear in the form of Tārā, as I described her earlier. Our body is made of brilliant green light, and vacuous like a tent of green silk. We are sixteen years old, smiling and beautiful, adorned with precious silks and jewels. We try to cultivate the feeling that our old personality with its faults and self-doubts has disappeared, vanished in the blueness, and now we are Tārā, infinitely compassionate. In our heart are the lotus, moon mat, and seed syllable, around which stand the letters of the mantra: *oṃ tāre tuttāre ture svāhā*, turquoise or jade green in colour.

The mantra has no rational meaning; it is a play on the sound of Tārā's name. Nonetheless, its associations are profound. According to one tradition, the mantra – being the sound-essence of Tārā (saviouress) – expresses all her powers of swift rescue. With *tāre* we are delivered from all worldly sufferings. With *tuttāre* we are liberated from conditioned existence itself. With *ture* we are prevented from falling into a one-sided view of Enlightenment. We are rescued from the danger of seeing nirvāṇa as something to attain for ourselves alone. *Ture* opens our heart to embrace the Bodhisattva ideal, of gaining Enlightenment in order to help all sentient beings do the same. (Thus we could say that *ture* ensures that we shall develop compassion, and hence that we shall eventually become Tārā, who is the quintessential experience of compassion. To try to gain Enlightenment purely for our own sake means we shall fail to achieve Tārā's blissful state.)

The mantra in our heart begins to rotate anticlockwise. (Mantras of male figures usually go clockwise, of female figures anticlockwise.) As it does so, rainbows pour from it, filling our vacuous green body and purifying it, until finally we sit like an elfin princess in the midst of the vast blue sky, our body filled with rainbows.

2 Making offerings to the Bodhisattvas and receiving their blessing

Having filled our body, the rainbows overspill from the crown of our head. They fan out, and begin rising up into the sky towards the zenith. At the end of each rainbow ray is a beautiful goddess. Each one bears an exquisite offering: flowers, lights, incense, water for washing, water for drinking, perfume, food, and music. Each offering is the most perfect imaginable. The goddesses rise ever higher through the clear sky, their long hair streaming behind them. Eventually, a brilliant light appears in the sky above them. It comes from a great gathering of Bodhisattvas, headed by Avalokiteśvara. In the forefront are the eight Great Bodhisattvas, whom we shall meet more fully in Chapter Seven.

The offering goddesses begin making their lovely offerings. They never exhaust what they have to give. Each offering is finer than the last. The great company of Bodhisattvas is delighted by the offerings. In response, they send down an empowering stream of light-nectar. This waterfall of happiness and good qualities cascades through the sky and falls onto the crown of our head. It enters our body of green light, and pours onto the seed syllable and mantra in our heart, causing them to shine even more brightly than before.

3 Rescuing sentient beings from suffering

Energized by the light-nectar, the mantra in your heart emits more light rays, which pass out through your body in all directions. The universe begins to fill with rainbows. Wherever a rainbow falls on a sentient being, all their sufferings, physical and mental, dissolve away. As this happens, they too begin to recite the mantra. The rainbows continue to range across the universe, relieving suffering everywhere.

At last, you are seated in the sky, still in a lovely light-body. The mantra never stops sounding in your heart. It is like a metabolic process. Human beings breathe; Bodhisattvas of the *dharmakāya* radiate ceaseless compassion from the mantras in their hearts.

Above your head, the beautiful offering goddesses never tire of making exquisite offerings to the Bodhisattvas. The Bodhisattvas never cease pouring down light-nectar into your heart. Around you in every direction the universe is filled with rainbows. All beings are joyfully chanting the mantra, and there is no suffering anywhere. Through her practice you have created Tārā's Pure Land for all beings.

White Tārā

Six

White Tārā – Cheating Death

All schools of Buddhism acknowledge the existence of magical powers. It is taken for granted that as your meditation practice deepens and your concentration improves you are quite likely to develop supernormal faculties. These are known as *siddhi* in Sanskrit (*iddhi* in Pali). In the Mahāyāna sūtras and in the Pali canon, psychic powers, including clairvoyance, clairaudience, telepathy, levitation, and memory of past lives, are frequently mentioned.

Buddhism has, in a way, never bothered too much about these things. Buddhist teachers, while accepting that they are signs that your mind is becoming more refined and concentrated, are usually more concerned that you should not become too excited by them and be diverted from your quest for Enlightenment. Philip Kapleau, an American Zen roshi, tells a story of a Zen disciple who was distracted in his meditation by visions of the Buddha, together with his advanced disciples, walking around him chanting sūtras. The only way in which he could dispel this distracting vision was by leaping into a barrel of icy water! The Zen approach is very uncompromising in this respect.

Buddhist tradition distinguishes sharply between mundane psychic powers, such as clairvoyance, and the highest *siddhi*, which is Enlightenment. It admits that mundane *siddhi* can be a useful addition to the range of 'skilful means' of a Bodhisattva. For example, telepathic knowledge of the thoughts of others may help a Bodhisattva to teach the Dharma more effectively. It also accepts that developing *siddhi* may encourage people, as they are signs of progress which can spur them on towards Enlightenment.

One magic power which is not given in the standard lists is longevity – the ability to live long. Though it is not included in the most common lists of *siddhi*, Buddhist yoga deals quite extensively with its development (as does Taoism). It is a useful power which is worth our consideration for two reasons. The first is simply that if you are trying to follow the Bodhisattva path, time is precious. The longer you can live, the more people you can lead to the Dharma.

The second reason concerns your motivation for spiritual practice. Generally speaking, there are two motivations that engage the energy of a human being. The first is the desire for survival, which can take more refined forms, such as the desire for success, riches, fame, sex, and security. Chasing after these is what the Buddha called 'the ignoble quest': being yourself impermanent and liable to suffering, you go in search of what is also impermanent and unable to provide lasting satisfaction. As we all know, despite its limitations the 'ignoble quest' can sometimes engage a great deal of our energy and interest. The other motivation is the desire for growth and development, the search for Enlightenment, which once attained is permanent and totally satisfying. This is what the Buddha called 'the noble quest'.

Spiritual practice consists in moving energy from the ignoble to the noble quest. This is no easy task. There may even be times when we fall between two stools. No longer so excited by the mundane, we have not yet been really sparked off by the possibility of gaining Enlightenment. So we may become a little becalmed and uninspired, and even feel we have less energy than our friends who have aims no higher than succeeding in business or saving up for new washing machines. If we keep practising the Dharma, though, we shall eventually plant our feet more firmly on the spiritual path, and find that we are deriving more energy from spiritual life than we ever did from the ignoble quest.

How wonderful it would be, though, if we could avoid this awkward transition! If we could find a method that engaged both our desire for spiritual development and the energy we usually invest in the struggle for survival, our practice would be really powerful and wholehearted. One way we can do this is by visualizing the figure of White Tārā. As a Bodhisattva, Tārā can rally all the parts of ourselves that are excited by the quest for Enlightenment. In addition, the white form of Tārā bestows the gift of long life upon her devotees. So those aspects of your being that are concerned with survival are also highly motivated to devote themselves to her.

The tradition of White Tārā as a conferrer of longevity goes back to ancient India. Her sādhana for developing this power was revealed to an Indian teacher called Vāgīśvarakīrti ('famed lord of speech'). As a result, he wrote a set of three texts called *Cheating Death*. These texts were passed on to Atīśa, one of the most inspiring of Buddhist masters, whom we met briefly in the previous chapter. As we saw, he was a great Tārā devotee. In fact he had visions of Tārā throughout his life. As one of his biographers says, 'From the time he was a child, he was preserved by Tārā, the patron deity of his former lives.' When he went to Tibet in 1042, he made sure that *Cheating Death* was translated into Tibetan.

Several important lineages of White Tārā practice have come down to us. One comes from Gampopa (Milarepa's 'heart-son' disciple, and founder of the Kagyu order), and was handed down through the Karmapas, the heads of the Karma Kagyu school of Tibetan Buddhism. Another line of transmission comes via the Dalai Lamas. (The first Dalai Lama, Gedun-drup, was very devoted to White Tārā.)

White Tārā performs her function of bestowing long life by herself, but also as part of a popular triad of 'long life deities' with Amitāyus (Tibetan *Tshepame*), whose name means 'boundless life', and Vijaya (Tibetan *Namgyalma*). Amitāyus is usually represented as a red Buddha, but is sometimes white, seated in meditation posture, holding a vase of the nectar of immortality surmounted by a sprig of leaves from the aśoka tree. (*Aśoka* in Sanskrit means without sorrows.) Unlike Amitābha, who is usually unadorned, Amitāyus wears the jewelled ornaments of a Bodhisattva. Vijaya, whose name means 'victory', is a white female figure, often with three heads and eight arms. Her distinguishing emblem is a small Buddha image held in her uppermost right hand. The Tibetans sometimes build stupas[31] for the long life of an important person, and these long-life stupas are often decorated with images of Vijaya.

The Buddhist view of factors influencing lifespan

We now need to ask the question: does the practice work? If so, how does performing the White Tārā sādhana increase your lifespan? Of course, there is no way of proving that it does, although many Buddhist yogins and meditators firmly believe in it. Nevertheless, modern medicine is finding increasing evidence of psychological factors underlying disease, so it is not unreasonable to suppose that a practice which produces concentrated and positive mental images and volitions will have a healing effect on the body.

Will-power is becoming increasingly recognized in the West as a factor in longevity. It has always been a firm tenet of popular songs and poetry that you can die of a broken heart or because you have nothing left to live for. A recent statistical survey showed that far more old people die shortly after their birthdays than in an equivalent period before it – suggesting that their determination to be at the celebration keeps them going.

A striking example of will to live is related by Antoine de Saint-Exupéry in his book about early aviators, *Wind, Sand and Stars*. A good friend of his, opening up mail flights in South America, crash-lands in the Andes. He is unhurt, but it is midwinter, he has no supplies, and he is far – too far – from civilization. He tries to walk out, scaling mountain passes at 15,000 feet, in temperatures twenty degrees below zero. After trudging for days, suffering bitterly from exposure and hunger, he finally falls on his face, and knows that the end has come. Blissful unconsciousness begins to envelop him.

Then he remembers that, under the terms of his life insurance policy, if his body is not found, his wife and family will have to wait four years before they can claim. He decides that if he can just manage to drag himself onto an exposed rock, some fifty yards away, there will be more chance of his body being seen from the air and recovered. Painfully, for his family's sake, he hauls himself to his feet. Three days later he staggers into a village. His will to survive – not for himself but for others – has carried him through ice and snow, hunger and biting winds, long after nature would have given up. He later said, 'I swear that what I went through, no animal would have gone through.' We must not underestimate the power of the human mind to carry the body beyond its natural limits.

From the Buddhist point of view, Vagīśvarakīrti says there are three reasons, or underlying conditions, which cause life to come to an end: exhaustion of life, exhaustion of merits, and exhaustion of karma. The White Tārā practice works on all three of these.

Exhaustion of life means that your physical vitality and energy are no longer sufficient to sustain life. You lose your physical robustness and cannot withstand disease. As we shall see later, one attribute of the White Tārā sādhana is that it is very calming and stilling. This meditation has the effect of concentrating energy and conserving and building up a reservoir of physical vitality.

Exhaustion of merits and karma both stem from the Buddhist view that you create the world in which you live. Each mental state calls into being an experience that is its objective counterpart. So if, as a human being, you no longer create sufficient positive mental states, or the volitions that caused you to be born as a human being are exhausted, then, according to the tradition, your life as a human being will come to an end. Through meditatively identifying yourself with White Tārā and her vast compassion for every form of life, you produce a great stock of merit and positive volitions. So by means of the sādhana you fulfil the conditions for long life.

Higher goals of meditating on White Tārā

By this point you may be thinking that the White Tārā practice is all very well, but it does not aim high enough. For a Buddhist, a long life may be very pleasant, but it is of little value in itself. After all, does not the *Dhammapada* say, 'Better than a hundred years spent without seeing the Deathless state, is one single day spent seeing the Deathless state.'[32]

While meditation on White Tārā may well give long life, developing longevity is not its central aim. Rather it is a tremendous bonus, which boosts the energy you can put into the meditation by enabling you to channel your lower, survival-oriented energies into it. What the practice is really about is clearly demonstrated by the White Tārā mantra: *oṃ tāre tuttāre ture mama āyuḥ puṇya jñāna puṣṭim kuru svāhā.*

This is the basic Tārā mantra we met with in the previous chapter, with an extra phrase inserted into it. There are many phrases which can be included in the basic mantra to make it effective for a particular purpose. This is the most common one, and is associated particularly with White Tārā. It means 'increase my life, merits, and wisdom'. Here we have a key to the practice. Through meditating on White Tārā we realize that human life (*āyus*) is valuable because it gives us the chance to develop merits (*puṇya*) and wisdom (*jñāna*), and to help others to do the same.

Dwelling upon long life also involves dwelling upon impermanence, dwelling upon death. So the practice subtly accustoms us to our own mortality. It makes us aware that even a long life must come to an end, and that it is vital to use whatever time we have to build our ship of death (as D.H. Lawrence calls it), and load it with the provisions of merits and wisdom.

Finally, if our practice goes deep enough, White Tārā bestows not just long life, but eternal life. We come to realize that even long life is not enough. We are really seeking, through performing the practice, to come to a place where there is no death. This search for the deathless state is the 'noble quest', the search for nirvāṇa. One of the epithets of Enlightenment is that it is the *amṛta* (Sanskrit, *amata* in Pali), which means deathless. After the Buddha had gained Enlightenment and decided to teach the Dharma, he said to Brahmā Sahampati, 'Open are the doors of the Deathless.'

This is the real goal of meditating on White Tārā: to help ourselves and all others to be liberated from the Wheel of Life (which is the Wheel of Death), and to attain the deathless state. The final and highest *siddhi* that White Tārā bestows is the attainment of Enlightenment itself.

Now we can see what we might call the central myth of White Tārā. Through her practice we gain long life. We buy time. We use that time to help ourselves and others to develop merit and wisdom. Through gaining merit and wisdom we fulfil the requirements for arriving at the deathless state, liberation, nirvāṇa, so we can then lead others out of saṃsāra to safety.

White Tārā and Green Tārā

White Tārā and Green Tārā are, in essence, the same figure. They both represent the quintessence of compassion. I practised the Green Tārā sādhana for nine years, and then took up White Tārā. In doing so I felt the external forms change, and there were some differences of emphasis in the sādhanas, but there was no essential change. Tārā is Tārā.

Apart from White Tārā's additional function as bestower of long life, the two practices do have a different feel to them. Green Tārā, with her right leg stepping down into the world, stresses the activity of compassion – like the spontaneous response of a mother to her child. White Tārā sits in full-lotus posture, still extraordinarily compassionate, but more centred, more still. These differences are reflected in the fact that while Green Tārā is often associated with Amoghasiddhi and his outward-going wisdom of infallible success, White Tārā is always regarded as belonging to the Lotus family of Amitābha, who could be characterized as the Buddha of meditation.

The other striking difference between the two figures is that White Tārā is adorned with seven eyes. As well as the usual two, she has an eye in the sole of each foot, the palm of each hand, and one in her forehead. So she is that form of Tārā which emphasizes that compassion must be wise. 'Fools rush in', but to help effectively you need to see clearly, to understand what is happening. White Tārā's seven eyes communicate that, to be fully effective, compassion must spring from awareness, from a balanced attitude, and ultimately from wisdom. So the feeling of the meditation is stiller, more contemplative, than that of the more active Green Tārā.

Aspects of White Tārā visualization

We have seen that there are several White Tārā meditation lineages which have continued to the present day. I am not going to talk about any sādhana in detail, rather I shall describe the figure of White Tārā more fully, and then comment on one or two features that appear in different sādhanas.

As usual, the figure of White Tārā appears out of the vast blue sky. The normal procedure is for everything to dissolve into Emptiness, then the white seed syllable *tāṃ* on a white lotus and moon mat appears out of the blue sky, after which you appear in the form of White Tārā. (Most White Tārā sādhanas involve self-visualization.)[33]

This threefold procedure – dissolution into the blue sky, appearance of the seed syllable, and arising in the body of the deity – has much symbolic significance, particularly in Highest Tantra. It symbolizes the purification of death, the bardo, and rebirth. The dissolution of ordinary appearances into the blue sky of Emptiness is a symbol for death. The seed syllable corresponds to the *manomayakāya*, the subtle body in which, according to some schools of Buddhism, the consciousness experiences the *bardo*, or 'intermediate state', between one rebirth and the next. Through the visualization you undergo the experience of death, bardo, and rebirth in a controlled and purified form. You happily let go of everything you know and care for, and 'die' into the blue sky of Emptiness. Then, out of your desire to benefit other beings, you manifest again in order to communicate the Dharma. First you appear in the subtle form of the seed syllable, then you take rebirth in the beautiful form of White Tārā to benefit the world. This procedure can be found, sometimes in a much-elaborated form, in many other sādhanas.

So what is the form in which you take rebirth in this visualization? You are seated, in the midst of the sky, on a white moon mat, spread on a white lotus throne. You are a young girl, sixteen years old, graceful and very attractive. Your body is made of white light, like sunlight on snow. You are dressed in delightful silks and jewels. Your legs are crossed in the full-lotus posture. Looking out from the upturned sole of each foot is a beautiful eye. Your right hand rests on your right knee, turned outwards to give to all beings. In its palm is another eye. Your left hand is held in front of your heart in the mudrā of bestowing protection. With it you hold the stem of a spray of white lotus flowers. This hand too has an eye in its palm. You have long sleek black hair which falls over your shoulders. Your compassionate smile drowns the world in happiness. In your forehead, placed vertically, is a seventh beautiful eye. Your body is empty, so that you feel as light as thistledown. You are surrounded by a great aura of white light in the shape of a full moon. Above your head, your guru, the Buddha Amitābha, sits in deep meditation, pouring love into the sky around him, as a shining ruby gives light. You try to generate the firm conviction that you are White Tārā, born from Emptiness for the sake of all living beings.

The sādhana then proceeds on its magical way. We shall not go into details. Instead, we shall look at some features of the figure of White Tārā. Every aspect of the visualized form of a Buddha or Bodhisattva has symbolic significance. It is the combination of the enjoyment of the figure's beauty with an understanding of its significance that makes these visualizations so potent. Sometimes the text of the sādhana will include a meditation in which we reflect on the import of every aspect of the figure we are visualizing. Let us take just a few features and see how this is done.

White Tārā is surrounded by a great circle of white light – a full moon aura. According to one interpretation, this symbolizes pacification and the increase of inexhaustible bliss. Through being endowed with this aura, White Tārā becomes a moon goddess. The moon is not only beautiful, it is peaceful and benign: shining gently on the world, easy to gaze at. Its being a full moon strengthens White Tārā's magical capacity for increasing things, for enabling them to grow to their fullest possible extent. The moon of our life, merits, and wisdom finally becomes complete, a perfect circle.

In her left hand she holds a spray of lotus blossoms, which are usually white, though they can also be the pale-blue night lotuses, known as *utpala*. There are three flowers, in various stages of development: one still a bud, one half open, and one fully open. In general, lotuses are symbols of growth and development – of leaving behind lower states and growing towards what is higher. The Tārā devotee aspires to leave saṃsāra behind and arrive at the perfect understanding of Enlightenment. However, these three lotuses can also be reminders of the empty, ungraspable nature of things. One traditional method for realizing this is to consider the nature of the three times – past, present, and future. The past, the fully open lotus bloom, has already passed away; the future, the bud, has not yet revealed itself; the present, symbolized by the half open flower, is as ephemeral as a flash of lightning.

White Tārā's seven eyes are mysterious. I have already mentioned that they suggest the need for compassion to be wise, to see clearly and objectively, otherwise it is mere pity or sentimentality. The explanation given in a meditation quoted by Stephan Beyer[34] is that the seven eyes stand for the four *brahma vihāras* and the three *vimokṣas*. The four *brahma vihāras*, as we have seen, are positive emotions which need to be cultivated as a basis for the development of the Bodhicitta. The three *vimokṣas* (or 'releases') are insights into different aspects of Reality.

In my own mind, however, I have come to associate the eyes with awareness. A basic Buddhist practice, without which you will not get very far with spiritual development, is known as 'guarding the gates of the senses'. This consists in trying to be aware, all the time if possible, of what you are taking in through the senses and how it affects you. Buddhism counts the senses as six. These comprise the usual five plus the 'everyday mind' which cognizes ideas, memories, and fantasies. So, for me, there are six eyes to stand guard over the senses, including the mind, to ensure that what they perceive does not catalyse anything unskilful. What about the seventh eye? Well, that must be the highest eye, in the middle of the forehead, which looks beyond the senses altogether, to perceive transcendental reality directly. So the seven eyes together suggest awareness permeating all levels of your being.

The eyes can be seen almost like breaches in the skin. This suggests that wisdom can break through in unexpected ways. Perhaps the symbolism of the seven eyes points to the fact that White Tārā's whole body is wisdom and awareness.

The alchemy of long life

One procedure, which occurs in several White Tārā sādhanas, makes clearer the symbolism underlying the practice. Having become Tārā in body and mind (i.e. in visualized form and holding to the 'divine pride' of thinking 'I am Tārā'), we then concentrate on the seed syllable *tāṃ* in our heart centre. Around it appears a great white wheel of the Dharma, lying flat, marked with several circles of mantras. Light pours from the *tāṃ* and passes out through our body to build up a series of concentric auras around us. By the end of this process we are seated in the middle of sphere upon sphere of light, each one a different colour, each bestowing a spiritual quality.

In this way we build up a mandala. We are seated in the middle of a circle of protection. The great auras of light ward off all hostile forces and influences, and attract everything that is beneficial to our Dharma practice.

Right at the centre of all these spheres of light, in the middle of the Dharma wheel with its circles of mantra letters, is the blazing white seed syllable *tāṃ*. It sits at our heart, at the core of our being, unmoving and radiant. This seed syllable is a symbol of our life, immobile and totally sheltered from harmful influences. Insulated by the protective mandala, we feel that nothing can affect us negatively. Our energy, our vitality, is concentrated and calm, and in this way our lifespan is enhanced.

However, the sādhana does more than just protect our life. If we practise it faithfully over time, a process of transformation begins, akin to an alchemical transmutation. While some alchemists have merely tried to change the nature of metals, there have been some in both West and East who have understood that true alchemy involves a transformation of the base metal of the everyday mind into the gold of higher states of consciousness. Similarly, in meditating on White Tārā, the mandala becomes a kind of alchemical crucible in which we concentrate and contain our energies so that they can be progressively refined and sublimated.

All the crude energy which is usually channelled into survival is gradually led into the practice, by the promise of long life, and transmuted into something higher.

All the energy that usually flows into sexual attraction and projection is led to fall in love with the bewitching beauty of White Tārā, or the compassionate strength of Amitābha, and thus to fall in love with Enlightenment. It too becomes refined.

Step by step, the process of alchemical transmutation proceeds. Our human emotions respond to the warmth and love radiated by White Tārā and Amitābha, and offer their energies, too, to the service of Enlightenment.

Our higher, artistic sensibility becomes totally involved in the process of the visualization. It is like watching a painter of genius taking the blue sky as a canvas to create a masterpiece that fills the cosmos. As our energies become more refined, so the colours and shapes become lighter and brighter. The universe reveals itself as a dance of light and colour.

As we continue practising the sādhana, higher and higher levels of energy are brought into play. Finally, one day, the *tāṃ* in our heart no longer symbolizes our mundane consciousness, cowering for safety behind protective shields of mantras and light, seeking to prolong itself indefinitely. At last the alchemical process is complete. The *tāṃ* at our heart is totally transmuted. From being a consciousness intent on long life and self-preservation, the *tāṃ* has been liberated. It has become the shining heart of a Bodhisattva.

It is a heart that is totally calm and still. We have truly become White Tārā, seated at the eye of the hurricane of saṃsāra, unmoved and unaffected. The *tāṃ*, our consciousness, is 'at the still point of the turning world' – the turning world of birth and death. From that heart, calm and free, rays of infinite compassion pour down upon the world. At this point the sādhana has done its transforming work, and what I have called the central myth of White Tārā has completely unfolded. However, it will take time for us to unfold all the elements of that myth, that sublime vision. So it is as well that White Tārā grants us long life, creates time for us to explore her practice, time to get to know her, time to arrive at her heart.

I think that, for me, the very first *siddhi* that White Tārā bestows is an appreciation of the importance of time. We need time to develop spiritually. It can take us many years to arrive at a point in our Dharma practice where we are on safe ground, and in no danger of slipping back. We need time to contact what is beyond time. We need time to practise the Bodhisattva path, time to take the Dharma out to a suffering world.

The first thing we see through the seven eyes of White Tārā – the fact which we see quite calmly, unrushed, and unruffled – is that even a long life is very short, and there is no time to lose.

Seven

The Eight Great Bodhisattvas

In the last five chapters we have encountered the Bodhisattvas whose names shine brightest in the dazzling firmament of the Bodhicitta: Avalokiteśvara, Mañjuśrī, Vajrapāṇi, and Tārā. However, just as the stars in the sky are countless, so are the great beings who are working to rescue the universe from suffering. In this chapter we are going to meet some of the other leading Bodhisattvas that one is likely to encounter in Buddhist visualization and devotional practice. In reading Mahāyāna sūtras, the roll of honour of Bodhisattvas who are mentioned as playing a part in the cosmic drama of Enlightenment runs to thousands. With most, we know little more than their names, but a few have played such a prominent part in Buddhist literature and devotional practice that they have a well-developed iconography. Rather than playing walk-on parts in Mahāyāna sūtras they have come to occupy centre stage and become characters in their own right.

Most of the best-known Bodhisattvas are included in the set of figures known as the eight Great Bodhisattvas, to whom the goddesses made their offerings in the Green Tārā sādhana in Chapter Five. Like the twenty-one forms of Tārā, they are sometimes represented together in Tibetan *thangkas*. All the figures are young and smiling. Each sits on a fully opened lotus throne, symbolizing that he has renounced the muddy darkness of the mundane and fully opened his mind to the sunlight of Enlightenment. Each is decked in the finery of an Indian prince, representing the endless spiritual riches he has gained through the practice of the six Perfections.

The eight Bodhisattvas are often depicted in the posture of royal ease. This posture demonstrates the huge enjoyment the Bodhisattva takes in his daunting task. He is working ceaselessly and untiringly for the benefit of a universe whose sufferings are unthinkable. Yet he does so with a joyful heart, relaxed and free. In fact, the Bodhisattva's work for sentient beings is sometimes referred to in sūtras as his *līlā*, which means play. The Bodhisattva plunges into saṃsāra with an inner reservoir of happiness, like an elephant plunging happily from one pool to another. He can do this because he sees things as they really are. He is in the world, but not of it. The total relaxation with which the Bodhisattva strains every nerve for living beings is summed up in the slightly languorous posture of royal ease.

Thangkas of the eight Bodhisattvas often give prominent positions to Avalokiteśvara, Mañjuśrī, and Vajrapāṇi, who together are known as the three family protectors (Tibetan *riksum gonpo*). Avalokiteśvara is the principal Bodhisattva of the Lotus family of Amitābha, Mañjuśrī that of Vairocana's Tathāgata family, and Vajrapāṇi that of the Vajra family of Akṣobhya. Together they form a symbolic triad. They represent the three main aspects of living beings, transformed and placed at the service of Enlightenment. Through Avalokiteśvara, Mañjuśrī, and Vajrapāṇi, feeling, intellect, and volition are transformed into compassion, wisdom, and spiritual power. There are several traditional ways of depicting the eight Bodhisattvas. In particular, their colours may vary. The most reliable way of identifying them is usually by their emblems. In describing those whom we have not yet met, I shall not attempt to give all the possible representational variations, I shall just describe one fairly common form in which they appear.

Samantabhadra

Samantabhadra (all good, Tibetan *Jangsem Kuntuzangpo*) is often white in colour, his right leg stretched out, his foot resting on a lotus flower. With his left hand he holds the stem of another lotus flower on which rests his emblem, the golden wheel.[35] Like Avalokiteśvara, he is particularly associated with compassion. Also like Avalokiteśvara, he appears in the *Saddharma Puṇḍarīka*, in chapter 26 (chapter 28 of the Chinese version), where he promises to protect the sūtra. The Buddha in turn promises to protect all those who recite the name of Samantabhadra, and declares that those who do so will gain merit equal to that of having visualized the Buddha.

Samantabhadra plays a crucial role in another great Mahāyāna sūtra, the *Gaṇḍhavyūha*. This sūtra, we have seen, tells the story of the spiritual quest of a young man called Sudhana, who is the archetypal pilgrim and searcher after truth. After meeting the Bodhisattva Mañjuśrī, Sudhana travels the length and breadth of India, trying to achieve the highest knowledge of Enlightenment. After meeting more than fifty great teachers, Sudhana's quest culminates in his meeting with Samantabhadra. He it is who finally gives Sudhana complete instructions for his development as a Bodhisattva. Through understanding Samantabhadra's teachings, Sudhana realizes that he is not different from all the Buddhas. His Enlightened consciousness and theirs interpenetrate without obstruction.

In the *Gaṇḍavyūha Sūtra*, Samantabhadra makes a famous set of vows, and worships the Buddhas with lavish offerings. This is often referred to in Tibetan pujas, where the participants imagine themselves making offerings as vast and extensive as those of Samantabhadra.

Samantabhadra became even more popular in China and Japan than in India. In Japan he is known as Fugen, and is commonly depicted green in colour, and riding a white elephant. Japanese tradition has him prepared to assume any form in order to help living beings. He is even represented becoming a courtesan in order to teach the Dharma to people who are unable to overcome their sexual craving.

Maitreya

Next we encounter a golden figure. He, too, is in the posture of royal ease. In his left hand is a lotus with a stupa – a Buddhist reliquary – rising up out of it. Looking at this figure we are scrying into the future. Here we have Maitreya ('friendly one', Tibetan *Jampa*) – the only Bodhisattva to have inspired widespread devotion in both Theravāda and Mahāyāna countries.

In the Pali canon, Maitreya (as Metteya, the Pali form of his name) is prophesied by the Buddha Śākyamuni to be the next Buddha to appear in our world-system.[36] He will be the last of the five Buddhas to gain Supreme Enlightenment in this *kalpa*, or aeon. Theravāda and Mahāyāna sources agree that at present he resides in the Tuṣita *devaloka* – a kind of heaven world. Far in the future, when the wave of teaching initiated by Śākyamuni, which we know as Buddhism, has died out, Maitreya will descend to Earth and take his last rebirth as a human being. He will rediscover the path to Enlightenment, covered over by the creepers of time and the briars of ignorance, and will proclaim the Dharma once more, 'for the benefit of gods and men'.

In anticipation of this event, he is frequently represented as a Buddha, and worshipped as such. Nāgārjuna, the founder of the Madhyamaka school, describes devotion to Maitreya as an easy, other-regarding path to Enlightenment. Maitreya is also the subject of a fervent paean at the end of Buddhaghosa's *Visuddhimagga*.

As a Bodhisattva, Maitreya appears in many sūtras. In the *Larger Sukhāvatī Vyūha* he is shown the Pure Land of Amitābha by Śākyamuni Buddha. In this sūtra, Maitreya is called by one of his other names, Ajita (unconquered). He also appears in the *Gaṇḍavyūha*. Earlier on in Sudhana's pilgrimage, before his meeting with Samantabhadra, he comes to a strange remote structure called the Vairocana Tower. This mysterious edifice refuses to yield its secrets to him until Maitreya appears.

Maitreya talks to Sudhana about the Bodhicitta, and at great length. He compares it to everything valuable and beautiful that it would be possible to imagine. Having prepared him in this way for the initiation he is about to receive, Maitreya just snaps his fingers. The door to the Vairocana Tower swings obediently open, and Sudhana walks in. He is stunned by what he sees. The tower is as wide as the sky, and full of precious things, but he hardly gives them a second thought, for the tower is also full of an infinity of Vairocana Towers, each full of precious things, and each with a young man called Sudhana standing inside. Maitreya is thus responsible for Sudhana's introduction into the transcendental realm in which all things interpenetrate (interpenetration being the main vision that the sūtra communicates).

According to tradition, this Bodhisattva is also the author of some commentarial works, known as the Five Books of Maitreya. These include the *Abhisamayālaṅkāra*, a brilliant summary of the *Perfection of Wisdom in 25,000 Lines*. However, modern scholars attribute these five works to Asaṅga or Maitreyanātha. There is no reason in principle, though, why the writer should not have been directly inspired by Maitreya to compose these works. Tradition has it that through deep meditation Asaṅga had a vision of the Tuṣita devaloka during which he received from Maitreya the teachings contained in the Five Books.

The stupa is just one of Maitreya's distinguishing emblems. He frequently holds a golden *dharmacakra* (wheel of the Dharma), or a sacred vase (*kalaśa*) full of nectar. This symbolizes the nectar of the Dharma, which he will one day pour upon the world.

Maitreya is often depicted in a pose known as *bhadrāsana*, which is virtually unique in Buddhist iconography. It looks as though he is sitting, legs down, on a chair or throne. However, this does not mean that the next Buddha will appear in the West, teaching from an armchair! It is meant to suggest that Maitreya is already preparing to descend into the world. In this posture he often holds one hand to his cheek, with three fingers extended, symbolizing the Three Jewels. He is gazing downwards, toward the world that he will one day enter to illuminate its darkness with his rediscovery of the Dharma. Perhaps, looking down from Tuṣita, he can just make out the words that have been imploringly carved and painted on rocks in many places in Tibet: 'Come, Maitreya, come!'

Kṣitigarbha

The next Bodhisattva we shall encounter is a seated green figure. His right hand touches the earth with its fingertips. The mudrā is redolent of absolute certainty. It is the security that comes from understanding the nature of existence, and resting upon the solid rock of the Dharma. In his left hand he holds a lotus, bearing a magic tree, which grants all wishes. This figure is Kṣitigarbha ('matrix of the earth', Tibetan *Sa nyingpo*). He represents the most moving aspect of the Bodhisattva's open-heartedness. Of all the realms of existence in which sentient beings suffer, Kṣitigarbha has chosen to work in the hells.

Kṣitigarbha

Buddhism has no conception of an eternal state of perdition. It finds no Creator God to judge living beings and cast them into the 'outer darkness'. However, being clear-sighted and based on experience, it acknowledges that through ignorance living beings do sometimes create hells for themselves. Some of these may be so dark and painful that without the compassionate intervention of a Bodhisattva to show them the path to safety, they would languish in misery for a very long time.

Like a hero fearlessly entering the underworld, Kṣitigarbha goes out of his way to encounter the wretched, the afflicted, the insane – those suffering all manner of physical and mental torment. He never tires of his work of rescue. Kṣitigarbha, we could say, is the Bodhisattva of seemingly lost causes. He is the embodiment of the supreme optimism of the Mahāyāna. He can face the most degraded and anguished sufferings of the universe, for he never loses sight of the Mahāyāna's vision of a cosmos in which every living thing, down to the worms under our feet, has come at last to Buddhahood. With what joy and relish he plunges into the fathomless darkness! With what infinite care he nurses those prostrate with suffering! What vastnesses of grim blackness vanish with the light of his compassion! Kṣitigarbha's is a heart vowed to eradicate the hells, single-handed if need be, even if it takes an eternity to achieve. If we could begin to imagine the feelings of that heart, the whole weighty structure of our own self-interest would shudder, as at a mighty earthquake, and fall asunder, never to be rebuilt.

Understandably, as time went on Kṣitigarbha attracted increasing numbers of devotees. In China and Japan especially he gained such popularity that eventually he was second only to Avalokiteśvara. In Far Eastern Buddhist art he is represented as a Sarvāstivādin monk, often depicted standing on a golden lotus. He is shaven-headed, with the monk's three-ringed staff in his right hand and a wish-fulfilling gem in his left.

One of the most popular sūtras in Chinese Buddhism is the *Sūtra of the Past Vows of Kṣitigarbha Bodhisattva*, which was translated into Chinese in the seventh century.[37] It describes how Kṣitigarbha works in multiple guises for the sake of those in states of extreme suffering. At one point, all these manifestations of Kṣitigarbha, weeping with compassion, reunite into one form and appear before the Buddha. They reassure him that he need not be concerned about beings in future ages who create much negative karma (the result of which would be to put them into hellish states). They assure him that they will rescue all such beings. The view of Kṣitigarbha is, 'If *I* do not help beings in the hells, who else will go?' and he is steadfast in his vow never to abandon them. Thus he also forms part of a set of four Bodhisattvas who are said in Chinese Mahāyāna Buddhism to embody the four basic qualities of the Bodhisattva: Mañjuśrī the great wisdom, Avalokiteśvara the great compassion, Samantabhadra the great meritorious deeds, and Kṣitigarbha the Bodhisattva's great vow to rescue all beings from suffering.[38]

In Japan he is known as Jizo. There he has taken on a number of functions. He is a kind of god of the roads, and protector of children. He is also the special patron of warriors (who may perhaps be in greater danger than most of us of falling into the hells).

Ākāśagarbha

Next we see a golden-yellow figure, also in royal ease, and holding his emblem, a wish-fulfilling jewel. This is Ākāśagarbha (Tibetan *Namkhai Nyingpo*), the 'celestial' counterpart of Kṣitigarbha. His name means 'matrix of the sky'. One text says this means that he possesses a great store of wisdom, boundless like space. He is associated with the dawn. He is the principal Bodhisattva of the Jewel family of Ratnasambhava.

The *Mahāvairocana Sūtra* – an important text in Far Eastern Buddhism – gives a different description of him. It pictures him wearing a white robe, and holding in his left hand a lotus with a large sword that radiates light. The *Sādhanamālā*, on the other hand, states that he is 'green as the sky', holding a wish-fulfilling jewel and making the gesture of supreme giving. Ākāśagarbha's spiritual significance is well brought out in a Chinese text:

> Suppose there is a Bodhisattva who has limitless riches, an immeasurable store of every kind of treasure, who generously makes large donations to people, especially to the poor and bereaved. Suppose that he opens his store to make offerings to those people as much as they want, and that he is thereby immensely satisfied. Like that rich man, does Ākāśagarbha Bodhisattva practise his meritorious acts.[39]

Ākāśagarbha is the perfect embodiment of the Perfection of Generosity, just as Kṣitigarbha personifies absolute altruism in its most heroic form.

Sarvanīvaraṇaviṣkambhin

We now come to a blue figure,[40] once more young and with a welcoming expression, who has as his emblem a moon on an open lotus, whose stem he holds. In some representations the moon is full, and in others it is a crescent.[41] This is Sarvanīvaraṇaviṣkambhin ('one who clears away all hindrances', Tibetan *Dripanamsal*). The word *nivaraṇa* here is the same as that used for the list of five hindrances that prevent one attaining dhyāna.[42]

In the Mahāyāna sūtras this Bodhisattva seems to have a connection with Avalokiteśvara. In a sūtra described by Alice Getty he expresses the desire to see Avalokiteśvara. So the Buddha sends him to Vārāṇasī where Avalokiteśvara miraculously appears to him. After this he never tires of praising Avalokiteśvara's qualities.[43]

In this list of eight Bodhisattvas Sarvanīvaraṇaviṣkambhin is occasionally replaced by Mahāsthāmaprāpta ('attained to great strength', Tibetan *Thuchenthop*). Like Vajrapāṇi, he is an embodiment of spiritual power. He appears in the *Amitāyur Dhyāna Sūtra*, as one of the two main Bodhisattvas (along with Avalokiteśvara) attendant on the Buddha Amitāyus in his Pure Land, Sukhāvatī. He is portrayed in Buddhist art as white or yellow in colour. His most frequent emblem is a spray of six full-blown lotuses, which he holds in his left hand.

The jewels in the lotus

In these chapters, looking at the eight Great Bodhisattvas and some forms of Tārā, we have met the Bodhisattvas most commonly depicted in Buddhist art. However, we have taken only a teaspoonful from the ocean of Bodhisattvas mentioned in the Mahāyāna sūtras.

We have had no space to do justice to some extraordinary figures. We have barely mentioned Vimalakīrti, the Bodhisattva who appears in the form of a layman, and whose trenchant insight adorns the *Vimalakīrti Nirdeśa*. We have not touched on the story of Sadāprarudita ('ever weeping'), whose story is movingly told in the *Perfection of Wisdom in 8,000 Lines*.

Neither have we been able to look at the extraordinary number of forms that the eight Bodhisattvas can take. To meet the needs of different systems of spiritual practice, they can change their colour, emblem, posture, or connection with a particular Buddha family. To take one example, the *Tibetan Book of the Dead* assigns the Bodhisattvas to Buddha families using a different scheme from the one I have followed in this book. For instance, Mañjuśrī appears in the bardo on the fourth day, as part of Amitābha's Lotus family.

These transformations, and changes of position in the mandala, should demonstrate that we are dealing not with conceptual pawns to be pushed around by the rational mind, but with potent spiritual energies. It is a useful first step to be able to recognize the different figures as they appear in Buddhist art. What is important, though, is not the ability to identify Bodhisattvas, but to identify *with* them. It is only when we do this that we shall begin to understand that a *thangka* is really a mirror – one that reflects the riches buried in the depths of our minds. The eight Great Bodhisattvas are eight great jewels hidden in the lotus of our heart. Each is a wish-fulfilling gem of a different radiance. Becoming aware of their existence will transform our understanding of what it means to be a human being. Shared with the world, their brilliance will dispel the darkness of suffering and ignorance for ever.

Notes

1 *The Life of the Buddha, Selections from the Pali Canon*, trans. Bhikkhu Ñāṇamoli, Buddhist Publication Society, 1978, p.52.

2 *The Holy Teaching of Vimalakīrti*, trans. Robert Thurman, Pennsylvania State University Press, 1976, p.50.

3 See *The Threefold Lotus Sūtra*, trans. Kato, Tamura, and Miyasaka, Weatherhill, 1982, pp.58–9.

4 Some Tibetan texts concentrate on seeing all beings as one's mother (e.g. Yeshe Tsondru's 'The Essential Nectar of the Holy Doctrine' in Geshe Rabten, *The Essential Nectar*, Wisdom, 1984, pp.225–30); others on seeing them as parents (e.g. see Jamgon Kongtrul, *The Torch of Certainty*, Shambhala, 1977, p.65). Clearly the point is that one should develop a feeling of kinship with all living beings.

5 Quoted in an article on 'Bodhichitta: the Perfection of Dharma' in *Wisdom*, magazine of the Foundation for the Preservation of the Mahāyāna Tradition, number 2, 1984, p.37.

6 See D.T. Suzuki, *Manual of Zen Buddhism*, Rider, 1956, p.14.

7 For a discussion of the power and effectiveness of mantras, see John Blofeld, *Mantras*, George Allen and Unwin, 1977, pp.42 and 96–104.

8 Here I am giving a slightly simplified version of the story as told by Geshe Wangyal in *The Door of Liberation*, Wisdom Publications, 1995, pp.60–1.

9 The ten heads are also said to represent the ten Perfections which the Bodhisattva practises as he or she progresses through the *bhūmis*, the stages of the Bodhisattva path.

10 This quotation comes from D.H. Lawrence's poem 'Song of a Man who Has Come Through'.

11 What I am giving here is a very simple form of self-visualization. For an example of a rather fuller meditation of the four-armed Avalokiteśvara see 'The Tantric Yogas of the Bodhisattva of Compassion' in *Selected Works of the Dalai Lama III*, compiler, ed., and trans. Glenn H. Mullin, second edition, Snow Lion, 1985, pp.204–10.

12 *The Tempest*, act iv, scene 1, lines 152–8 in the *Arden Shakespeare*.

13 From the *Saddharma Puṇḍarīka*, quoted in *Buddhist Texts Through the Ages*, ed. Edward Conze, Harper and Row, 1964, pp.195–6.

14 The philosophers I know who have read this paragraph have winced, and tried to convince me that there are some exciting developments taking place in Western philosophy. I hope they are right.

15 Buddhists and other non-Christians do not use the abbreviations AD – 'Year of our Lord' – and BC. They refer to years under this accepted dating convention as either CE (Common Era) or BCE (Before Common Era).

16 *Svayambhūpurāṇa*, ed. Hariprasad Sastri, Bibliotheca Indica, 1900, p.166 et. seq.

17 'Manjushri' by Étienne Lamotte, *T'oung Pao 48* (1960), pp.60–84.

18 There is another Buddhist figure particularly associated with learning and music. This is the goddess Sarasvatī, who also occupies an important place in Hinduism. She is usually represented as two-armed and white in colour, and holding a *vina* – an Indian stringed instrument.

19 Sangharakshita, *The Three Jewels*, Windhorse Publications, 1998, p.166.

20 This is a much simplified sādhana, based on the structure of 'The Sādhana of the Srijñā-Guṇaphala-nāma Stuti' by Siddhacarya rDo-rje mTshon-cha and Bhadanta 'Jam-dbYans mKhyen-brTse'i dBan-po, translated literally by John Driver and edited by Sangharakshita, private edition, 1977.

21 Repetition of the syllable *dhīḥ* is considered by Tibetan Buddhists a potent way of purifying and developing the intellectual faculties. In Geluk monasteries monks can sometimes be heard reciting it repeatedly at the end of debates.

22 *Ambaṭṭha Suttanta, Dīgha Nikāya* 3.

23 In Buddhist tradition a yakṣa is a kind of powerful demon, somewhat akin to an ogre. See *The Sūtra of Golden Light,* trans. R.E. Emmerick, Luzac, 1970, p.66.

24 These are the first three of the list of the ten fetters (Pali *saṃyojana*). According to the Hīnayāna view, these ten comprise all the negative states that must be overcome in order to attain Enlightenment. The first three have to be broken for transcendental insight to arise.

25 *Saṃyutta Nikāya* 5.2.

26 Though the story of Tārā being born from Avalokiteśvara's tears is well known, I have been unable to trace any canonical source for it. Alice Getty (*The Gods of Northern Buddhism*, Charles E. Tuttle, 1962) asserts that the Green Tārā was born from tears from the left eye, and the White Tārā (see Chapter Six) from tears from the right. I have described the legend in terms of Green Tārā as scholars agree that this form was the original one, of which others were later developments.

27 For a translation of this Tantra, with an introduction to it, see Martin Willson's *In Praise of Tārā*, Wisdom Publications, 1986, pp.44–85.

28 Ibid., p.107.

29 Ibid., p.34.

30 Sādhana of Green Tārā received by Sangharakshita from Chatrul Rimpoche by way of oral transmission.

31 The stupa (Tibetan *chorten*) is one of the most important of all Buddhist symbols. Beginning as funeral mounds in which relics of the Buddha were enshrined, they developed into three-dimensional symbols for Enlightenment and the stages of the path leading to it.

32 *Dhammapada*, chapter 8, verse 15.

33 An exception, written by Lama Zopa, appears in Janice Dean Willis, *The Diamond Light*, Simon & Schuster, 1973.

34 See Stephan Beyer, *The Cult of Tara*, University of California Press, 1978, p.449.

35 Alice Getty (in *The Gods of Northern Buddhism*, Charles E. Tuttle, 1962), says that he can be yellow or green. There are many systems of iconography relating to these figures, and their colour is not a reliable feature by which to identify them. The best way to make a positive identification is by looking at their emblems. Even these are not one-hundred-per-cent reliable, however – Getty gives the main symbols associated with Samantabhadra as the wish-fulfilling jewel, the scroll, and the mace.

36 *Cakkavatti-Sīhanāda Sutta*, the 26th sutta of the *Dīgha Nikāya* (DN iii.76).

37 Available in English as *Sūtra of the Past Vows of Earth Store Bodhisattva – collected lectures of Tripitaka Master Hsuan Hua*, trans. Bhikshu Heng Ching, Buddhist Text Translation Society, 1974.

38 These four Bodhisattvas are also associated in some forms of Chinese Buddhism with the four elements: Kṣitigarbha with earth, Avalokiteśvara with water, Samantabhadra with fire, Mañjuśrī with air or space.

39 'Ta-fang-teng, ta-chi-ching' quoted in G.P. Malalasekera (ed.), *An Encyclopaedia of Buddhism*, Government of Ceylon, 1964, vol.1, p.342.

40 According to Alice Getty (p.106), Sarvanīvaraṇaviṣkambhin is white or grey.

41 Compare, for example, the line drawings in *Heart of Wisdom*, Tharpa, 1986, p.97, and *Mystic Art of Ancient Tibet*, p.149, Shambhala, 1987, icon 149.

42 These five are (1) desire for sense experience, (2) ill will, (3) sloth and torpor, (4) restlessness and anxiety, (5) doubt. These are what prevent the mind from attaining higher states of consciousness, and they have to be overcome for the experience of positive concentration on a skilful object of concentration to arise. See Kamalashila, *Meditation: The Buddhist Way of Tranquillity and Insight*, Windhorse Publications, 1996.

43 Getty (pp.106–7) states that this incident is mentioned in the *Saddharma Puṇḍarīka*, but this is incorrect. It is most likely to be in the *Kāraṇḍa-Vyūha*, to which I have not had the opportunity to refer.

Illustration Credits

Colour plates

PLATE ONE Vajrapāṇi – wrathful form by permission of the Rupa Company, Kathmandu

PLATE TWO Green Tārā wall painting by Dhammachari Devaraja.

PLATE THREE White Tārā thangka by permission of Dhammacharini Varadevi.

PLATE FOUR Maitreya thangka by permission of Dhammachari Maitreya.

PLATE FIVE Prajñāpāramitā by permission of Dhammachari Padmakara. Photographed by Dhammachari Padmakara.

PLATE SIX Vajrasattva thangka by permission of Dhammachari Chintamani.

PLATE SEVEN Padmasambhava thangka by permission of Dhammachari Kulamitra.

PLATE EIGHT Milarepa thangka by permission of Dhammachari Maitreya.

Black and White Illustrations

PAGE 12 Detail of Avalokiteśvara thangka by permission of the London Buddhist Centre.

PAGE 20 Detail of Avalokiteśvara wall painting by Dhammachari Devaraja.

PAGE 26 Mañjuśrī drawing by Dhammachari Aloka.

PAGE 40 Vajrapāṇi drawing by Dhammachari Aloka.

PAGE 54 Detail of Green Tārā thangka. See Plate Two.

PAGE 70 White Tārā thangka by permission of ITBCI School, Kalimpong. Photographed by Dhammachari Dhammarati.

PAGE 90 Kṣitigarbha thangka painted by Dhammachari Amritasukha.

Glossary

AMṚTA Nectar, which symbolizes the blissfulness of practising the Dharma. It literally means deathless.

ANIMAL REALM The realm of existence in which consciousness is dominated by the struggle for survival and the basic drives for food, sex, and sleep. It may refer to actual animals or to human beings in such states of consciousness.

ARHAT Originally a term of respect for someone who had gained Enlightenment. In Mahāyāna and Vajrayāna Buddhism it came to represent someone who settled for the lesser ideal of personal emancipation from suffering, in contrast to the Bodhisattva (q.v.).

ASURA Similar to the Titans of Greek mythology, asuras are powerful and jealous beings who are prepared to use force and manipulation to gain their own ends. In the Wheel of Life (q.v.) they are represented as warring with the gods. They may be seen as objectively-existent beings or as symbols for states of mind sometimes experienced by human beings. Female asuras are called asurīs and are represented as voluptuous. Asurīs play on their seductive charms to gain their own ends.

BARDO (*Tibetan*) The 'state between' two other states of being. In particular the intermediate state between one life and the next.

BHŪMI One of a series of stages of development which a Bodhisattva passes through as he or she moves toward Enlightenment. It literally means ground.

BODHICITTA The compassionate 'desire' (based not on egoistic volitions but on insight into the true nature of things) to gain Enlightenment for the benefit of all living beings. More technically, it can be divided into absolute Bodhicitta, which is synonymous with transcendental wisdom, and relative Bodhicitta – the heartfelt compassion that is the natural consequence of an experience of absolute Bodhicitta.

BODHISATTVA A being pledged to become a Buddha so as to be in the best position to help all other beings to escape from suffering by gaining Enlightenment.

BRAHMA VIHĀRAS, FOUR loving-kindness (*maitrī*), compassion (*karuṇā*), sympathetic joy (*muditā*), and equanimity (*upekṣā*).

BUDDHA A title, meaning one who is awake. A Buddha is someone who has gained Enlightenment – the perfection of wisdom and compassion. In particular, the title applied to Siddhārtha Gautama, also known as Śākyamuni, the founder of Buddhism.

BUDDHA FAMILY The five main groupings into which every aspect of existence – both mundane and transcendental – is divided in Tantric Buddhism. The blueprint for these groupings is provided by the mandala of the five Jinas (q.v.).

BUDDHAS, FIVE Another name for the five Jinas (q.v.).

CITTAMĀTRA Literally 'Mind Only'. A school of Mahāyāna Buddhism, initiated by the fourth-century Indian teacher Asaṅga, which denies that there is any ultimate distinction between mind and matter. Also known as the Yogacāra school.

COMPLETION STAGE The second of the two stages of Highest Tantra (q.v.). It focuses on advanced practices designed to concentrate and channel the most subtle energies of the psychophysical organism, in order to bring about the speedy attainment of Enlightenment.

CONDITIONED EXISTENCE See saṃsāra.

DEVA A long-lived being who experiences refined and blissful states of mind. Devas thus inhabit a heavenly realm. These realms can be interpreted as objective or as symbols for states of mind in which human beings can dwell.

DHARMA A word with numerous meanings. Among other things it can mean truth or reality. It also stands for all those teachings and methods which are conducive to gaining Enlightenment, and thereby seeing things as they truly are, particularly the teachings of the Buddha.

DHARMACAKRA The 'Wheel of the Truth'. A large golden wheel, symbolic of the Buddha's teaching.

DHARMAKĀYA Literally 'body of truth'. The mind of a Buddha. The Enlightened experience, unmediated by concepts or symbols.

DHYĀNA A state of supernormal concentration on a wholesome object. It may occur spontaneously, but is generally the fruit of successful meditation practice. Buddhist tradition recognizes different levels of dhyāna, each one increasingly refined and satisfying.

EMPTINESS See śūnyatā.

ENLIGHTENMENT A state of perfect wisdom and limitless compassion. The only permanently satisfying solution to the human predicament. The achievement of a Buddha.

ESOTERIC REFUGES Those Refuges (q.v.) which are matters of direct personal experience, embodied in the guru, yidam, and ḍākinī by the Buddhist Tantra.

FAMILY PROTECTOR The chief Bodhisattva (q.v.) associated with a Buddha family (q.v.), as in the set of the three family protectors: Avalokiteśvara, Mañjuśrī, and Vajrapāṇi.

GELUK By far the largest of the four main schools of Tibetan Buddhism, founded in the fourteenth century by Tsongkhapa. It emphasizes ethical discipline and training in clear thinking as a basis for meditation.

GENERATION STAGE The first of the two stages of Highest Tantra (q.v.). It focuses on the development of the vivid visualization and experience of oneself as a deity.

GOING FOR REFUGE The act of committing oneself to the attainment of Enlightenment by reliance on the three Refuges (q.v). Also refers to the ceremony by which one formally becomes a Buddhist.

GURU A person who through teaching and/or personal example helps other people to follow the path to Enlightenment.

HELL REALM A state of extreme physical or mental suffering, the hell realms may be understood as objective states into which one can be reborn, or as symbols for states of extreme distress experienced in the course of human life. Buddhism has no concept of a permanent state of perdition.

HIGHEST TANTRA The most advanced of the four levels of Buddhist Tantra. It consists of the Generation and Completion stages (both q.v.).

HĪNAYĀNA The 'lesser way' or 'lesser vehicle'. Buddhist schools who do not advocate the Bodhisattva ideal. Though in common use among Mahāyāna and Vajrayāna Buddhists, the term is regarded as pejorative by the Theravāda school (q.v.).

HUMAN REALM The state of being 'truly human' – characterized by a balanced awareness of both the pleasant and painful aspects of life, and a capacity to co-operate and empathize with other human beings. In Buddhism this state is regarded as the best starting-point from which to enter the path to Enlightenment.

HUNGRY GHOST A class of being (*preta* in Sanskrit) too overcome by craving to gain satisfaction from any experience. The idea can be interpreted literally, or symbolically as a state of mind sometimes experienced by human beings. Pretas are represented in Buddhist art with large stomachs and pinhole mouths.

JEWELS, THREE The Buddha, Dharma, and Sangha (all q.v.). The three highest values in Buddhism.

JINAS, FIVE A very important set of five Buddhas, often represented as interrelated in a mandala (q.v.) pattern. They each embody a particular Wisdom (Sanskrit *jñāna*) – an aspect of the Enlightened vision. Jina literally means 'conqueror'.

KADAM A school of Tibetan Buddhism springing from the Indian teacher Atīśa in the eleventh century. It no longer survives, but its teachings were taken over by the Gelukpas, who are sometimes referred to as the New Kadam school.

KAGYU One of the four main schools of Tibetan Buddhism, founded in the eleventh century by Gampopa. It emphasizes meditation and has produced many successful solitary meditators.

KARMA Literally 'action'. Simply stated, the so-called 'law of karma' says that our willed actions (mental and vocal as well as physical) will have consequences for us in the future. 'Skilful' actions arising from states of love, tranquillity, and wisdom, will result in happiness. 'Unskilful' actions, based on craving, aversion, and ignorance, will produce painful results.

LAMA (*Tibetan*) see guru.

LAM RIM (*Tibetan*) 'Graduated Path'. A system of teaching founded by the Indian master Atīśa in which all the stages of the path to Enlightenment are laid out in a very clear and systematic manner. Each of the four main schools of Tibetan Buddhism has produced Lam Rim texts.

LOWER TANTRAS The first three of the four main divisions of Buddhist Tantra (q.v.): action (Sanskrit *kriyā*), performance (Sanskrit *caryā*), and union (Sanskrit *yoga*).

MADHYAMAKA A school of Mahāyāna thought founded by the Indian teacher Nāgārjuna. It is characterized by a denial that concepts can ever accurately describe Reality.

MAHĀYĀNA The 'great way' or 'great vehicle'. Those schools of Buddhism that teach the Bodhisattva ideal – of selfless striving to gain Enlightenment so as to be in the best possible position to help all other living beings to escape from suffering.

MAITRĪ Universal friendliness or universal loving-kindness. One of the four *brahma vihāras* (q.v).

MANDALA A word with various meanings in different contexts. In this book it means a pattern of elements around a central focus. Ideal mandalas are often used as objects of meditation in Buddhist Tantra.

MANTRA A string of sound-symbols recited to concentrate and protect the mind. Many Buddhist figures have mantras associated with them. Through reciting their mantra one deepens one's connection with the aspect of Enlightenment which the figure embodies.

MĀRA The Buddhist personification of everything that tends to promote suffering and hinder growth towards Enlightenment. It literally means 'death'.

MERITS The positive states generated through the performance of virtuous actions, which predispose one to encounter happy and fortunate circumstances.

MUDRĀ Can be the general term for a Tantric emblem. In this book it is used in its sense of a hand gesture imbued with symbolic significance. In Tantric Buddhism it can also refer to a female consort.

NIRVĀṆA The state of Enlightenment, the cessation of suffering. For the Mahāyāna (q.v.) it became a lesser ideal – a state of blissful happiness in which one could settle down rather than working compassionately to help all other beings to attain the same happy state.

NYINGMA The oldest of the four main schools of Tibetan Buddhism, deriving its original inspiration from the Indian teacher Padmasambhava, who went to Tibet in the eighth century.

PALI CANON The collection of teachings of Buddha Śākyamuni and some of his close disciples, originally written down in Pali, and regarded as authoritative by the Theravāda school (q.v.).

PERFECTION (Sanskrit *pāramitā*) The main positive qualities that the Bodhisattva (q.v.) strives to develop. A positive quality only becomes a *pāramitā* in the full sense when it is imbued with transcendental wisdom. The six perfections constitute the most important list of positive qualities in Mahāyāna (q.v.) Buddhism: generosity, ethics, patience, effort, meditation, and wisdom.

PRAJÑĀPĀRAMITĀ The 'Perfection of Wisdom', direct intuitive insight into the true nature of things, through which one overcomes ignorance and thereby the principal cause of suffering. In Tantric Buddhism it is also the name of a female deity who is the embodiment of the Perfection of Wisdom.

PRECEPT One of the ethical trainings recommended by the Buddha and other Buddhist teachers. There are various lists of precepts, but the most fundamental is a set of five Buddhist ethical trainings. Put in negative terms they involve working to refrain from (1) harming living beings, (2) taking the not-given, (3) sexual misconduct, (4) untruthfulness, and (5) dulling the mind with intoxicants. In positive terms this means striving to develop (1) loving-kindness, (2) generosity, (3) contentment, (4) truthfulness, and (5) awareness.

PURE LAND A realm created through the meditative concentration and meritorious actions of a Buddha, in which beings can be reborn. In a Pure Land, conditions are totally favourable for progress towards Buddhahood. Also, the schools of Buddhism whose practice centres on being reborn in such realms.

REALMS, SIX A classification of all the possibilities for rebirth within conditioned existence. They are the realms of the devas, asuras, humans, animals, hungry ghosts, and beings in hell (all q.v.). The six realms are pictorially represented in the Wheel of Life (q.v.).

REFLEX Certain of the five Jinas can appear in a second form, which demonstrates another aspect of their Wisdom. This second form is sometimes described as the 'reflex' of the Jina.

REFUGE One of the things on which Buddhism believes it is wise to rely. The three Refuges – the Buddha, the Dharma, and the Sangha – are common to all forms of Buddhism. The Esoteric Refuges (q.v.) are peculiar to Buddhist Tantra.

RIMPOCHE (OR RINPOCHE) (*Tibetan*) An honorific title for a Tibetan Buddhist master – especially one who is believed to be the rebirth or emanation of a previous highly-developed Buddhist practitioner. It literally means 'precious one'.

ROSHI (*Japanese*) A practitioner of Zen (q.v.) who has received *inka*, or certification of his readiness to teach, from his own teacher. More generally, a Zen Buddhist master.

SĀDHANA A general Sanskrit word for one's personal religious practice. More specifically, a Buddhist Tantric practice usually involving visualization and mantra recitation. The written text of such a Tantric practice.

SAKYA One of the four main schools of Tibetan Buddhism, deriving its original inspiration from the Indian Tantric master Virupa.

SAMĀDHI A state of deep and concentrated meditation, usually conjoined with direct insight into the true nature of things.

SAṀSĀRA The cyclic round of birth and death, characterized by suffering and frustration, which can only be brought to an end by the attainment of Enlightenment.

SANGHA In the widest sense, the community of all those who are following the path to Buddhahood. As one of the Refuges (q.v.) it refers to the Ārya or Noble Sangha – those Buddhist practitioners who have gained insight into the true nature of things and whose progress towards Buddhahood is certain. In other contexts the term can refer to those who have taken ordination as Buddhist monks or nuns.

SEED SYLLABLE Subtle sound-symbols through which Enlightened beings can communicate the Dharma to those on advanced stages of the path to Enlightenment. They are often visualized in Tantric meditation.

ŚĀKYAMUNI The 'sage of the Śākyans', an epithet of Siddhārtha Gautama, the founder of Buddhism.

SIDDHI Supernormal attainments (such as telepathy) gained through meditation, especially using the methods of Buddhist Tantra. Enlightenment is the supreme *siddhi*.

SHINGON (*Japanese*) The Tantric Buddhism of Japan, introduced from China in the ninth century by the master Kukai.

ŚŪNYATĀ Literally 'emptiness' or 'voidness'. The ultimate nature of existence, the absolute aspect of all cognizable things. The doctrine of śūnyatā holds that all phenomena are empty (*śūnya*) of any permanent unchanging self or essence. By extension, it can mean the transcendental (q.v.) experience brought about by direct intuitive insight into the empty nature of things.

SKANDHAS, FIVE A classification of all the processes that make up the self or person. Used in Buddhism to demonstrate that there is no unchanging soul or self.

SKILFUL MEANS See upāya.

SPIRITUAL In this book, spiritual means concerned with the development of higher states of consciousness, especially with the path to Enlightenment. In this context it has nothing to do with spirits or spiritualism.

STUPA Originally a mound or structure built to commemorate a Buddha or other highly-developed person, and often containing relics. It became a symbol for the mind of a Buddha.

SUBTLE BODY A subtle counterpart to the physical body, made up of refined psychophysical energies, which is visualized in some forms of Tantric meditation.

SŪTRA Literally 'thread'. A discourse given by the Buddha, or by one of his senior disciples and approved by him, and included in the Buddhist canon. *Sūtra* is Sanskrit; the Pali is *sutta*.

TANTRA A form of Buddhism making use of yogic practices of visualization, mantra, mudrā, and mandalas (all q.v.), as well as symbolic ritual, and meditations which work with subtle psychophysical energies. Also the Buddhist texts, often couched in symbolic language, in which these practices are described.

TATHĀGATA A title of the Buddha. Can mean 'one thus gone' or 'one thus come'. A Buddha goes from the world through wisdom – seeing its illusory nature. He comes into it through compassion – in order to teach living beings how to put an end to suffering.

THANGKA (*Tibetan*) A Tibetan religious painting.

THERAVĀDA The 'School of the Elders' – the form of Buddhism prevalent in Thailand, Burma, and Sri Lanka.

TRANSCENDENTAL (Sanskrit *lokottara*). Experience that goes beyond the cyclic, mundane round of birth and death. The experience or viewpoint of an Enlightened being.

UPĀYA The skilful methods compassionately employed by Buddhas and others to interest people in the Dharma and encourage them to follow the path to Enlightenment.

VAJRA A ritual sceptre, which symbolically combines the qualities of both diamond and thunderbolt.

VAJRAYĀNA The 'way of the diamond thunderbolt' – Buddhist Tantra (q.v.) of India and the Himalayan region.

VISUALIZATION A common method of Buddhist meditation, involving the use of imagination to create vivid symbolic forms.

WHEEL OF LIFE A graphic representation of the whole process through which craving, hatred, and ignorance cause living beings to circle in states of unsatisfactoriness. It includes depictions of the six realms of devas, asuras, humans, animals, hungry ghosts, and beings in hell (all q.v.), which together represent all the mental states unenlightened living beings can experience.

YĀNA A 'way' or 'vehicle' which can be used for attaining Buddhahood. One of the great streams of thought and teaching (embracing a number of schools) that have appeared in the development of Buddhism. (*See* Hīnayāna, Mahāyāna, Vajrayāna.)

YIDAM (*Tibetan*) A Buddhist meditational deity embodying an aspect of Enlightenment. The term is sometimes reserved for meditational deities visualized in Highest Tantra (q.v.).

YOGA A Sanskrit word meaning union. In Buddhist Tantra it refers to a method of meditation or physical exercise designed to bring about spiritual development.

YOGACĀRA See Cittamātra.

YOGIN A male practitioner of yoga. The term is applied particularly to adepts of Buddhist Tantra.

YOGINĪ A female practitioner of yoga; a female Tantric adept.

ZEN (*Japanese*) A school of Mahāyāna Buddhism found mainly in Japan and Korea. 'Zen' is derived from the Sanskrit word *dhyāna* meaning 'meditation', and Zen places great emphasis on the practice of seated meditation. It aims not to rely on words and logical concepts for communicating the Dharma, often preferring to employ action or paradoxes.

Selected Reading

General

David L. Snellgrove, *Indo-Tibetan Buddhism*, Serindia, 1987.
Blanche Christine Olschak and Geshe Thupten Wangyal, *Mystic Art of Ancient Tibet*, Shambhala, 1987.
Marilyn M. Rhie and Robert A.E. Thurman, *The Sacred Art of Tibet*, Thames and Hudson, 1991.

Chapter One

Paul Williams, *Mahāyāna Buddhism*, Routledge, 1989.
Sangharakshita, *A Survey of Buddhism*, Windhorse Publications, 2001.
Sangharakshita, 'The Bodhisattva: Evolution and Self-Transcendence', in *The Priceless Jewel*, Windhorse Publications, 1993.
Shantideva, *A Guide to the Bodhisattva's Way of Life*, trans. Stephen Batchelor, Snow Lion, 1992.
Geshe Rabten and Geshe Ngawang Dhargyey, *Advice from a Spiritual Friend*, Wisdom Publications, 1984.
Jamgon Kongtrul, *The Great Path of Awakening*, Shambhala, 1987.

Chapter Two

The Threefold Lotus Sūtra, trans. Kato, Tamura, and Miyasaka, Weatherhill, 1982.
John Blofeld, *Bodhisattva of Compassion (The Mystical Tradition of Kuan Yin)*, Shambhala, 1978.
H.H. the Dalai Lama, *Aryasura's Aspiration and a Meditation on Compassion*, Paljor Publications, 2002.

Chapter Three

Chanting the Names of Mañjuśrī, trans. and annotator Alex Wayman, Shambhala, 1985.

The Holy Teaching of Vimalakīrti, trans. Robert A. Thurman, Pennsylvania State University Press, 1987.

Chapter Four

Sangharakshita, *Buddha Mind*, Windhorse Publications, 2001.

Chapters Five and Six

Stephan Beyer, *The Cult of Tara*, University of California Press, 1978.

Martin Willson, *In Praise of Tārā*, Wisdom Publications, 1986.

Index

Windhorse Publications is a Buddhist publishing house, staffed by practising Buddhists. We place great emphasis on producing books of high quality, accessible and relevant to those interested in Buddhism at whatever level. Drawing on the whole range of the Buddhist tradition, our books include translations of traditional texts, commentaries, books that make links with Western culture and ways of life, biographies of Buddhists, and works on meditation.

As a charitable institution we welcome donations to help us continue our work. We also welcome manuscripts on aspects of Buddhism or meditation. To join our email list, leave your address on our website. For orders and catalogues log on to www.windhorsepublications.com or contact:

Windhorse Publications	Perseus Distribution	Windhorse Books
11 Park Road	1094 Flex Drive	P O Box 574
Birmingham	Jackson TN 38301	Newtown NSW 2042
B13 8AB	USA	Australia
UK		

Windhorse Publications is an arm of the Friends of the Western Buddhist Order, which has more than sixty centres on four continents. Through these centres, members of the Western Buddhist Order offer regular programmes of events for the general public and for more experienced students. These include meditation classes, public talks, study on Buddhist themes and texts, and bodywork classes such as t'ai chi, yoga, and massage. The FWBO also runs several retreat centres and the Karuna Trust, a fundraising charity that supports social welfare projects in the slums and villages of southern Asia.

Many FWBO centres have residential spiritual communities and ethical businesses associated with them. Arts activities are encouraged too, as is the development of strong bonds of friendship between people who share the same ideals. In this way the FWBO is developing a unique approach to Buddhism, not simply as a set of techniques, but as a creatively directed way of life for people living in the modern world.

If you would like more information about the FWBO please visit the website at www.fwbo.org or write to

London Buddhist Centre	Aryaloka	Sydney Buddhist Centre
51 Roman Road	14 Heartwood Circle	24 Enmore Road
London	Newmarket NH 03857	Sydney NSW 2042
E2 0HU	USA	Australia
UK		

ALSO FROM WINDHORSE PUBLICATIONS

The Breath

by Vessantara

The breath: always with us, necessary to our very existence, but often unnoticed. Yet giving it attention can transform our lives.

This is a very useful combination of practical instruction on the mindfulness of breathing with much broader lessons on where the breath can lead us. Vessantara, a meditator of many years experience, offers us:

* Clear instruction on how to meditate on the breath
* Practical ways to integrate meditation into our lives
* Suggestions for deepening calm and concentration
* Advice on how to let go and dive into experience
* Insights into the lessons of the breath

The Breath returns us again and again to the fundamental and precious experience of being alive.

144 pages
ISBN 1 899579 69 9
£6.99/$10.95/€10.95

An interesting in-depth investigation into the art of breathing.
Yoga magazine

The Heart

by Vessantara

The Heart offers ways to discover your emotional potential through an exploration of the practice of loving-kindness meditation.

Vessantara has practised this meditation for over thirty years. Here he shares his experience, gently encouraging us to unlock what is in our hearts and helping us to gain greater enjoyment from life. Among other benefits, using the exercises and meditations in this book you can:

* Increase your emotional awareness
* Feel more at ease with yourself
* Become kinder and more open-hearted
* Discover how to be more patient
* Engage more spontaneously with life.

The Heart provides clear instruction and helpful suggestions for those new to meditation as well as more experienced practitioners.

176 pages
ISBN 9781 899579 71 6
£6.99/$10.95/€10.95

—the art of meditation series—

Buddhism: Tools for Living Your Life

by Vajragupta

This book is a guide for those seeking a meaningful spiritual path while living everyday lives full of families, work, and friends. Vajragupta provides clear explanations of Buddhist teachings and guidance applying these to enrich our busy and complex lives.

The personal stories, exercises, reflections, and questions in this book help transform Buddhist practice into more than a fine set of ideals. They make the path of ethics, meditation, and wisdom a tangible part of our lives.

> *In this book I have attempted to convey a feeling for what a 'Buddhist life' might be like – the underlying flavour, or ethos, of such a life. I hope I have made it clear that this way of life is possible for anyone – whatever their background and experience. My aim is to make the teachings as accessible and relevant as possible, and to give you some 'tools' with which to live a spiritual life.*

"I'm very pleased that someone has finally written this book! At last, a real 'toolkit' for living a Buddhist life. His practical suggestions are hard to resist!"

Saddhanandi, Chair of Taraloka,
named Retreat Centre of the Year 2006 by *The Good Retreat Guide*

192 pages
ISBN 9781 899579 74 7
£10.99/$16.95/€16.95

Creative Symbols of Tantric Buddhism

by Sangharakshita

Tantric Buddhism is concerned with the direct experience of who we are and what we can become. For the Tantra this experience cannot be meditated by concepts, but it can be evoked with the help of symbols.

This is a thorough and informative introduction to:

- ★ The symbolism of colour, mantras, and the mandala of the five Buddhas
- ★ The Tibetan Wheel of Life – a map of our mind and emotions
- ★ Figures of the Tantric tradition – Buddhas, Bodhisattvas, dakinis, and the archetypal guru
- ★ The symbolism of ritual objects and offerings
- ★ Confronting and transforming our fear of crisis situations and death

224 pages, with b&w illustrations
ISBN 1 899579 47 8
£10.99/$19.95/€19.95

OTHER BOOKS IN THIS SERIES

A Guide to the Buddhas
by Vessantara

Why does Buddhism refer to so many Buddhas? Who are they and what can they tell us about ourselves? In this book we meet the historical and archetypal Buddhas who form part of the rich symbolism of Tibetan Buddhism. This is an informative guide for those new to Buddhism and a handy reference for more experienced practitioners. Vessantara, with more than thiry-five years of meditation experience, combines the power of story-telling with practical guidance and brings the Buddhas and their visualization practices to life.

176 pages
Price £11.99/$18.95/€18.95
ISBN 978 1 899579 83 9

A Guide to the Deities of the Tantra
by Vessantara

Tantric deities? Who are they and what do they do? This book provides a fascinating insight into a subject that has captivated the imagination of many but remains mysterious and exotic to all but a few. This volume focuses on the deities whose mantra recitation and colourful visualizations lie at the heart of the Tantra. We meet goddesses of wisdom, the prince of purity, the lotus-born guru Padmasambhava, and ḍākinīs – wild-haired women who dance in the flames of freedom. The peaceful and the wrathful urge the reader to break through to wisdom, pointing out the true nature of reality with uncompromising vigour.

192 pages
Price £11.99/$18.95/€18.95
ISBN 978 1 899579 85 3